The Skatepark of Ulaanbaatar 2002

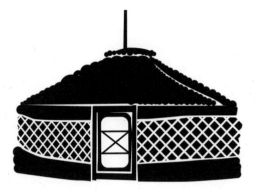

carhartt

The Skatepark of Ulaanbaatar 2004

Verlag für Bildschöne Bücher, Berlin 2007
http://bildschoene-buecher.com
ISBN 978-3-939181-04-0
1st Edition

Printed by Jütte-Messedruck Leipzig GmbH in Germany
DVD printed by EDD Bizz GmbH in Germany

Bibliographic information published by: Die Deutsche Bibliothek.
Die Deutsche Bibliothek lists this publication in the Deutsche Nationalbibliographie.
Detailed bibliographic data is available in the internet at: http://dnb.ddb.de

The content of this book and DVD is a compilation of personal views
and does not necessarily reflect the opinion of the producer and publisher.

A SKATEBOARD TRIP TO MONGOLIA

his book and the associated film capture a visual experience through the capital of Mongolia and its surrounding landscapes. Based on a photo of a giant skatepark in the center of Ulaanbaatar that was taken two years beforehand, a group of eleven skateboarders took the challenge in July 2004 and found themselves face to face with the ruins of the park, that had been torn down just three weeks earlier.

A voyage through the joy and pain of skateboarding, random architecture, endless countryside and the knowledge of how to ollie on dirt.

Photography:
Pontus Alv, Sweden | Alexander Basile, Germany | Bertrand Trichet, France.

Additional Photography:
Quentin de Briey, Spain | Henrik Edelbo, Denmark | Johannes Hempel, Germany.

MONGOLIAN TYRES
Documentary Film by Henrik Edelbo.

Featured Skateboarders:
Pontus Alv, Sweden | Scott Bourne, USA | Quentin de Briey, Spain | Tom Derichs, Germany
Julian Dykmans, Belgium | Vincent Gootzen, The Netherlands | Geoffrey van Hove, Belgium
Hugo Liard, France | Chris Pfanner, Austria | Kenny Reed, USA | Muki Rüstig, Austria.

FOREWORD *by Scott Bourne*

I think the thing about skateboarding that has happened to me over the last ten or so years is "The Journey". What I mean is that skateboarding is no longer only about skateboarding. It's about so many other things that occur along the way. In actuality, skateboarding is merely the fuel for adventure. The idea might have been "let's go here or let's go there to skate", but the truth is there is an entire story that happens along the way. That story to me is why I continue to skateboard, not because I want to. Long ago I stopped wanting to skateboard, for no other reason than my body keeps telling me not to skateboard. I hurt all the time. The reason why I say all that is to get to this: As far as the book is concerned, I think we should include everything that was shot that has relevance to the journey that we all embarked on, not knowing what the hell we would really find. By that I mean that the book should speak to the reader about life. Not just skateboarding. Of course, skateboarding is our lives. This is what we do. But a photo of some skateboarder walking through the ghettos of Ulaanbaatar on a dirt road is just as important as a photo of him at the spot. Many times the media destroys the story with glory. Well, there was no glory in Mongolia. We worked for every photo that any of us got and every single one of these people involved, I feel certain, had his life changed. So what I mean to say is that the book should include all of these other strange experiences which the desire to skateboard brought to us all.

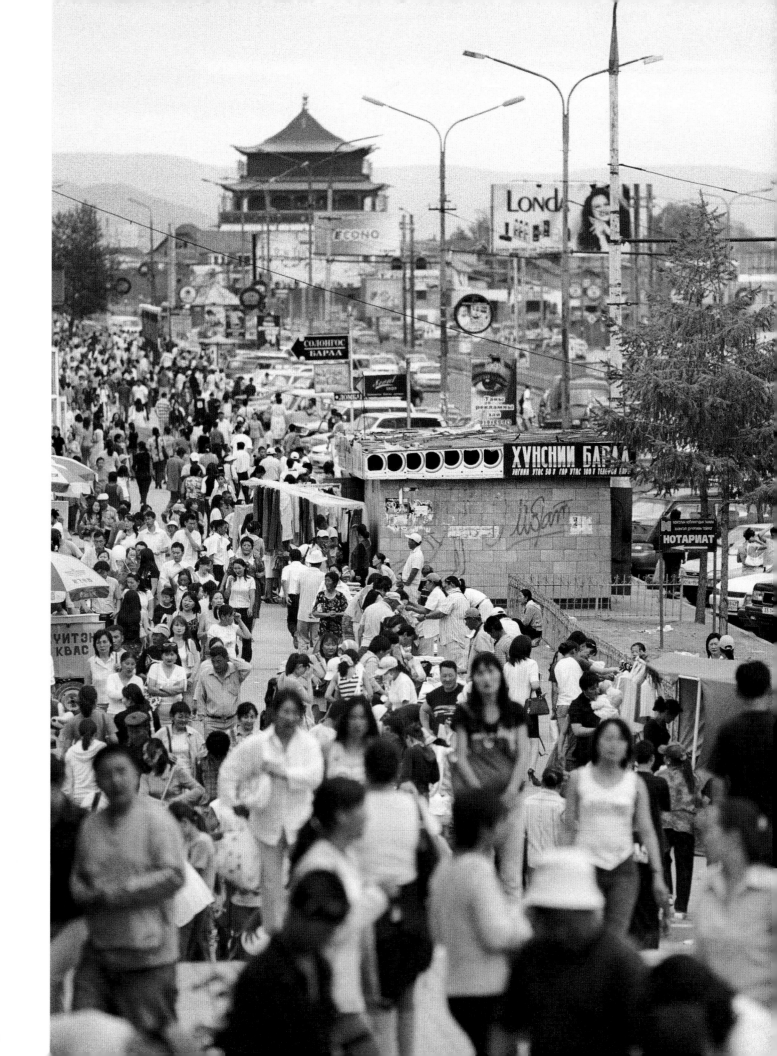

KIDS SNAPPING

The photographs on the following ten pages have been shot
by a school class in Ulaanbaatar.

DEMODAY

July 15th 2004, 11:00h–18:00h,
Sükhbaatar Square, Ulaanbaatar.

77

THE DIARY *by Scott Bourne*

July 1ˢᵗ 2004 | ## Charles de Gaulle Airport, Paris – France

Standing in the airport, the flight board reads Cairo, Casablanca, Rome, Chicago, Barcelona, New York, Milan, San Francisco, Berlin, Amsterdam, Togo, Singapore, Moscow, Bejing, Ft. Worth, Montréal and about a hundred other cities I've never heard of. I stare up at the flight board and try to figure out which one of these destinations is mine, try to figure out which is home. In the next 48 hours I will have been in Paris, Amsterdam, Berlin, Moscow and finally in Ulaanbaatar, Mongolia. The thoughts that run through your mind on the evening you lay down to go to sleep just before one of these trips, the first thoughts you have in the morning when you wake up. The things you see in your head, the people, the places – loved ones dead and gone – places so deep in the memory that they are distorted by merely trying to recall them. You remember what you choose to remember and often you choose to distort that memory. You have traveled so far and experienced so much that often when you return home – wherever that may be – you can no longer relate to the ones who are closest to you. They look different, and you do, too, and what has now become so important to you becomes meaningless when you find that you cannot explain it to those you love. Your experience often creates a certain solitude that becomes useless to express. Here you are with all these wonderful gifts of which you cannot give. Alone, alone, alone.

July 4ᵗʰ 2004 | ## Ulaanbaatar – Mongolia

I watched the sunset out the window of the plane till it created what seemed to be an infinite orange line across the sky. Staring out the window the line spread as far as one can see in either directions in varying shades of orange and red and just hung there. Unable to sleep on planes, I continued to read the book I brought – glancing from time to time out the window at this bright line that hung in the air and burned the sky in such magnificent colours. At times the cloud formations across the skyline seemed to form imaginary cities and silhouetted them with this great sunset. For what seemed like hours this great red-orange line hung in the sky and soon I realized that we were racing the sun along the edge of the earth. My sense of direction thrown off by this idea. I could not figure out which way was east and which way was west. For the great line in the sky fell out of the left hand side of the plane and it appeared as if we were headed east over Russia. Then, before I knew it, the same sky which I had watched slowly darken into the orange-red glow across the skyline – seemed to brighten, and the sun began to rise again from nowhere. Slowly the light filled the sky and with it came the dawn. Less than an hour later we were on the ground. Outside the airport I had no idea what would await me.

July 4th 2004 | ## Chez Bernard cafe – Mongolia

We were greeted at the airport by Juliane Schmidt. She is a German archaeologist working here in Mongolia and our connection with the city. She was young attractive and seemed very happy at our arrival. She was with two men who were Mongolian, one a politician. Before we even exited the airport he told me that the elections were yesterday and the communist had lost the election. To him and many people, Mongolia is now without government. Upon exiting the airport we noticed two large cows grazing on the lawn across from a mostly dirt parking lot. We spent the next three hours waiting for customs to give us the packages we had shipped from Germany for our trip. Late in the afternoon we arrived at Juliane's flat where she lived with her boyfriend Jean-Mathieu. He works with the Mongolian people aiding them in agricultural development. According to him the people are quite reluctant to learn. It seems that these people have a diet composed almost completely of meat, but have no great problem with nutrition. He is a French man. The two of them have been here for about three years. We ate and talked and they gave us a brief history about the country and the people.

July 5th 2004 | ## 3AM

Outside you can hear the packs of wild dogs running wild through the ghetto. The place is filled with neglect. I cannot sleep. Today we went to the Buddhist Temple here in Ulaanbaatar. These places have been some of the most sacred places I have seen in all my travels. When I saw the temple here earlier today I could not believe my eyes. The place was so run-down. Drunken men were pushing each other around in the mud out front and then fist fighting. Their faces scarred and deformed from drunkenness and poverty. Disrespect on the lawn of the temple. It was then that I was hit with the strange depression of Ulaanbaatar. Mothers sending their children over to us to beg for money, the sky clouded with coming rain and just out in front of me the faded temple of this once powerful dynasty that seems to be destroyed by the outside influence of the western world – a world that they cannot reach nor can reach them. Off the balcony one can see the wasteland sunset of poverty over the sea of yurts and housing projects side by side in the dawn of a once powerful dynasty. I want to leave, but where does one go from here? No matter what Mongolia will forever be stuck in my mind like a childhood tragedy – or the rape of my innocence, which becomes more and more brutal each time my enemy enters me. But still I seem to walk and talk and find a way to laugh in the face of this tragedy which is also a part of my history. At night the sky is filled with stars, but I do not dare to make a wish.

July 7ᵗʰ 2004 | ## Ulaanbaatar

Yesterday was our last day before the rest of the team's arrival. Quentin and myself met with Juliane and Mathieu for lunch. From there we went to the countryside with one of their friends who works for the forestry. Jerome – and one of his friends from Holland, as well as a Mongolian girl. We drove out of the city, but I am unsure which direction from Ulaanbaatar. Slowly the slums of the city disappeared behind us and were replaced by the countryside and its sights. Sheep, goats, cattle and horses roomed the countryside. At points they stand in the road slowing traffic. The further we get from the city, the better I feel. The conversations are scattered by language. Once completely out of the city, my heart and soul begin to calm. Rock formations jut up out of the earth forming mountains and valleys. The green grass of Mongolia covers the countryside like a fine carpet. Green in varying shades. All equally beautiful. It lays across the hills and valleys growing up onto the mountain side where it transverses into trees. These small trees are scattered over the mountainside thinning towards the top. Cattle or yak are thick in packs across the mountainside. We stop the car to take photographs, and one is allowed to go so close to the yak, that he can almost touch them. They are slightly larger than cattle, with long hair that falls almost to the ground. Horns jut out from their heads where they are firmly mounted to the skull giving the animal a fearful look – in spite of this look they seem very calm, peaceful, even humbled. Quentin and myself laugh at their strange appearance. Alongside the road we see camels and small ground squirrels but do not stop. Jerome tells us we are headed to the river Tuul, which is a boundary for the Mongolian people. After close to two hours we are near and Jerome pulls the jeep over to let the Mongolian girl out at some horses. Then we continue another ten minutes till we reach the river's edge. There is a small creek which we must cross before we come to the river which lies in the distance. Upon placing my feet to the water I find it icy cold. So cold I can feel a shock run through my entire body. I feel calm and clean and slowly wade to the other side as the mountains look down on me and the water changes its path as it wraps around my body. The small island between the river and me is composed of long flat river rocks, and a large dead tree turned grey in the sweat of summer sun. Ahead of me the river is wide and strong. Its waters are so clean that it appears shallow. As I enter my feet slip with the current and I struggle for my balance. Its strength reminds me that I am one man, a small man in God's domain. All around me is his skin the way he meant it. In my past lays the cities of my demise – above are the large birds who sail the sky as if it were the untamed ocean. I go under and do not wish to come up, but my lungs and my feet force me upright again. My body shivers but it is not from the cold, but the cities locked in my memory.

Down the river I see two women coming towards us on horseback, one is the Mongolian girl who came with us. They stop and she stays on the small island with us as the other woman leads the two horses back down the river.

As I sit on the dead tree on the island it seems as if the very rotation of the earth has come to a halt. San Francisco does not exist, neither does Paris, Ulaanbaatar or anything made by human hand, just me, my friends and the Garden of Eden as it was intended. From time to time I see my life in this strange light and here in this moment all I know is the earth.

Tonight – as the sun began to fall and I made my way back to the flat with Quentin and Pontus – the city seemed unreal – hellish even. Drunken men, passed out on the sidewalk and side streets. Young Mongolian women in high heels and tiny skirts, looking for money or simply a way out. I do not look like these people, or walk, talk, or think like them, and I find myself alone again – in that aloneness I find this place like any other place on earth – I AM ALONE – and yet, I am among friends, and together we find our way back to the ghetto wasteland of our flat and lock ourselves in as if we were precious metal. Gold or silver, as if our lives had more worth than those we had just seen passed out on the street or those who sell their bodies. But we are as they – lost and alone in the ghettos of humanity.

July 9th 2004 | ## Ulaanbaatar

The night before last was unbearable. At about twelve o'clock at night I heard a faint scream. I was lying in bed on a mattress on the floor. I was exhausted and half asleep. Then the scream came again. This time I came fully awake. From then on out our apartment was filled with the most insane screaming I have ever heard. The screams were amplified by my mattress, which was directly on the floor. The screaming was so intense that it was unbelievable. I then called out to Quentin in the next room: "Do you hear that?" From there we both went to the balcony. The screaming was coming from two levels down. It echoed from the windows of the apartment out into the wasteland ghetto of Ulaanbaatar where it then bounced back at us from the opposite buildings. The screaming was unbelievable due to the nature of its horror.

Down below and up above us we saw people sticking their heads out windows and off their balconies, but no one did anything or even said anything. The screaming went on for close to an hour and a half. At one point it stopped for about ten minutes. In those ten minutes I was struck with a strange relief. I was overcome by the idea the suffering had come to an end and even in my mind I had considered that the end might have been death. I was confused that I could conceive such a thing. I became really uneasy with myself. Then, just like before, the screaming began again. I began to dress, fully ready and willing to go down and knock on the door of the apartment. As I was dressing, Quentin's face was overcome with what looked like fear. "What are you going to do?" "You can't go down there!!!" It wasn't hard for him to talk me out of it, but as I lay in bed that night – listening to the screams slowly fade away – I felt a great disappointment in myself as well as Quentin. What does it mean when someone screams like that and no one comes. It was a call for help, a desperate scream for help – what if that were my scream, or the scream of a loved one, and no one came. What do we really fear, and is not our safety selfish. As I lay there sleepless for another night I could not help but think of the Nazi's and their crimes against humanity – crimes that people ignored. Ignoring such crimes is in some way just as great of a crime as the committing of such crimes. Often I feel alone. I am aware that my judgment is not always the best and yet I feel like it is instinctive to want to help someone who calls out to me, and to not help one must use a certain level of self deception – a rationalization of personal importance over the importance of another, but what does it mean when we override an impulse or instinct to help another? I feel very foreign here. Never have I felt so far from people in my life. I feel further from these people than I ever have from the Americans and for the first time in my life I feel fortunate to be from America, even if I do not approve of the American way – I am definitely fortunate.

July 12th 2004 | ## Ulaanbaatar

In the evening I stand out on the balcony and watch the nuclear sunset overtake the city. Small nomadic homes lay in the dust beside giant modern buildings. It looks like a burnt down Brooklyn 2004. A man on horseback with his child comes down a street as a car honks its horn and speeds by, pulling a storm of dust behind it. The man with his child seems unaffected. In the distance I can see cranes and smoke stacks emptying themselves into the air. The sky forming a radioactive rainbow of oranges and purples, in the same skyline a Ferris wheel turns slowly on the horizon. Old meets new in a clash that goes seemingly unnoticed by the Mongolian people. To walk the streets of this city a man can easily find himself embarrassed to be alive, to be human, and at the same time all a man needs to do is take a short car ride into the countryside, to once again feel privileged to be alive, to be human, and take the air into ones lungs. If there is black and white or night and day, it is easily visible from this height – here high in the mountainous regions of Mongolia.

July 14th 2004 | ## Ulaanbaatar

Pontus and I made dinner at the flat tonight and ate on the back balcony overlooking the city. To the left, the green, green mountains of Mongolia. But in front, the skyline polluted with industry. To the right, the project style housing. The conversation was slow and easy and for the first time, I admired the city, the country. Everything seemed to stop for a moment; the horror of this place's poverty became invisible. I felt ok with the place and it seemed to accept me as well. The foreigner, the outsider, the man among men in a mad world – mad world.

The most insane ideas come into my mind as I walk these streets. The children with their perfect smiles playing in a mud puddle that the rain has brought and a car has irritated into muck. The perfect dress and high heels of a Mongolian woman as she walks through this dusty wasteland with such elegance, her perfect round face and soft brown skin illuminate the darkness of poverty. The lack of violence in this place leaves one feeling quite hopeless – it's as if no one cares, as if no one wants out. The state of apathy here is at an all time high. No one is fighting for more – no one seems to want more.

July 16th 2004 | ## Ulaanbaatar

For the last three days I have been sick in the stomach. Incisive diarrhea and constant stomach pains. Last night our entire group met for dinner at a Korean restaurant. It was a nice place with a patio that looked out upon one of the country's temples. I had a good appetite for the first time in days – but when the menu arrived there was nothing vegetarian. When traveling like this I am more than willing to eat things I would not normally eat in my own country – but my stomach had been so bad I decided I should eat elsewhere.

July 17th 2004 | ## Ulaanbaatar

This city is so dark and disgusting and at the same time the children wear such light and innocence about their dirty faces. A few nights ago I had been out with Lars. We were leaving a bar where I had spent at least fifty euros on drinks with the boys. It was nice and I felt good to buy a round. But as Lars and myself stood alone on the street to flag a cab – a small boy came up to us. The child was no more than four years old. His arms and legs so thin that they look like sticks. He was barefoot in torn jeans and no shirt. In his arms he held a small girl clinging to him around the neck. He held onto her with one arm as he held out his other hand for money. The girl's naked bottom exposed to the night air, not yet ripe enough for sale. But I knew as I looked of these children – their destiny. Never before have I been so uncomfortable with the world. Lars and myself just looked at each other with equally lost faces. Although I have been told not to give these children money, I did, and Lars and myself decided not to talk about it. I felt it was a good decision and we got into a cab and rode off – deeper into the night. In the darkness of the cab I felt tears on my face and although I feel certain Lars noticed, he did not speak of it. By the end of the night we were both drunk – maybe secretly trying to delete the children from our memories. I think I did not write about it because I did not want to remember it. But now – on this night – it comes back to me. Outside on the street the dogs are barking and it seems strange that I have traded the morning birds of Paris for the rancid howling of the dogs of Ulaanbaatar. I step in and out of these selves. All of which added together create the sum of the man I am – changeable – changed, different, a new. But only a man – nothing more.

July 18th 2004 | ## Karakorum – Mongolia

Yesterday, I awoke early and made my way to the post office in Ulaanbaatar. I was to meet the entire group at eight for the trip to Karakorum and wanted to post some letters before I left. I had felt quite sick for the last couple of days and was fundamentally against making the trip at all. The roads through the country are very bad and even in a good jeep they are quite upsetting to the stomach. However there was a Monastery in Karakorum which I wished to see, so I joined the group. The group was divided between one bus and a jeep. I rode in the jeep for most of the journey. A journey which I was told was about six hours, turned out be nine. Staring out the window of the jeep one sees the beauty of Mongolia. It doesn't take long to feel the direct and intense change from the city to the country. The landscape is painted in varying shades of green with mountains on all sides. Horses, cows, sheep and goats roam the countryside free and wild. Rivers cut through the earth like the exposed veins of creation. The earth itself becomes the earth again, no longer the perverse interpretation of the human being. The sky falls infinite across the air in deep blues and pure whites. Up ahead is a single road that stretches out into the distance without turns or exits. There is nowhere to go but forward, for the knowledge of Ulaanbaatar will keep you from looking back.

Small camps of yurt or ger, spring up along the road and fade again into the distance, till finally the bumpy worn out asphalt turns to dust and dirt. And although it forces one to travel a bit slower, I must admit that the dirt seemed much smoother than many of the paved roads we have known so far. After close to two hours of dirt I am surprised to see that we have once again reached a paved road – a road very much unlike the one we began our journey on. This road is quite smooth, almost perfect and our vehicle is allowed to travel at normal speeds for almost an hour, before of course, the road turns to shit once more.

The journey has taken us along the edge of the Gobi desert. For the most part, it has been hot and miserable. A constant consumption of water without urination. The last hour of the trip I am switched into the bus where I find the ride much softer and a bit more spacious.

As the bus comes into Karakorum I can see the Monastery of Erdene-Zuu, which was not destroyed by communist rule, even though its people were. Its high wall stands strong surrounding the monastery and gives one an immediate sense of resistance as well as spiritual freedom. I wonder what god stood by the side of these monks as they resisted the rule of the communist.

Passing the monastery one becomes aware of the valley we have just entered. All around us are large green hills and mountains, their grassy shores polka-dotted with grazing sheep, cattle, goats and horses. A village stretches out along its base. Our bus pulls into a tiny camp where we quickly place our belongings into separate yurts and head to the river for a swim before nightfall. At night I sleep soundly for the first time on this trip. I am hit with a complete awareness of how spiritual this place is. I am certain it is the most beautiful place I have ever been in all my travels – not just because of the sensation it gives the eye but the sensation one gets in his heart and spirit.

July 21ˢᵗ 2004 | Chez Bernard cafe – Ulaanbaatar

Made the ride back from Karakorum in only six hours. Three hours shorter than the journey there. Kenny and myself spent all day yesterday going all over the city trying to get the necessary items for a Visa through Russia. After three trips to the Embassy we were still denied. We were told to come back tomorrow. Today we have all the documents and tickets for travel – if they deny us the Visa now they are just hateful people. I have had diarrhea for over two weeks now and have noticeably lost weight. Although I have had an incredible experience here – I cannot wait to leave this country. Outside the heat is melting the streets turning this city into the desert it was meant to be.

July 23rd 2004 | Trans Siberian Rail – Mongolia

My last night in Ulaanbaatar was spent with the entire group over good food at Taj Mahal, an Indian restaurant in the city. Conversations seem heated – all revolving around our time here. As I looked down the table at the seventeen faces that sat before me, I could see my tiny experiences with each person in the group. As I stared at them I couldn't help but feel as if we had all shared in an amazing experience that none of us were quite aware of yet – it would only be time that would reveal and cause us each to remember the trip in separate scenes, which would amount to a shared experience. I imagined the pieces of the trip that I had enacted but not seen. Just as I had seen the scenes of others' lives that they were unable to see. I perceive that these experiences have brought me closer to these men in such a short amount of time that it shall not matter if I ever see any of them again – their faces will remain burned in my memory till the end.

I left the restaurant before any of the others, giving off subtle but easy farewells. I am appalled by the idea of endings, even in the great novels, I know that long after the author writes the words "THE END" – that his life goes on somehow scarred and changed by the chapter he's laid down – till he inevitably picks up his pen again. As I rode back to the apartment on that evening I thought of the changes Juliane had told me about in her interview – changes Ulaanbaatar had been through in the years she had been there. Looking out the cab window at the cars incisive palpitations, the horns barking back and forth – the dusty streets crowded with head lights, and people crossing on their soft flesh suicide. I couldn't help but imagine these poorly constructed buildings evolving into skyscrapers. The next Hong Kong, the next Tokyo, the next CIVILIZATION to rise out of the dust and destroy itself – another neon circus cut in the earth – another worthless place to visit – but as it stood, it had its own strange beauty – a beauty I felt privileged to see and at the same time relieved to escape.

CAPTIONS

Cover   Muki Rüstig | Frontside 50-50 | Ulaanbaatar.
         Photographer: Alexander Basile
"I don't know how, but this is it. The spot describes skateboarding in Ulaanbaatar at it's best. The NO SPOT spot. And after each try the rail got more twisted. Muki Rüstig 50-50. And forget about riding away clean…" (Alexander Basile)

Inside Cover Ulaanbaatar Skatepark | Ulaanbaatar | Summer 2002.
         Photographer: Johannes Hempel
"This picture was taken during an archaeological excavation trip to Mongolia in 2002. Before the excavation started I spent some days in Ulaanbaatar, the capital of Mongolia. As a skateboard fanatic my friend Batsaikhan took me to this place. All of a sudden I was standing in front of this huge skatepark. But it looked more like an old forgotten dinosaur than a skateable park to me. We entered an apartment from a friend who lived just next to the park to get a better overview. That day nobody could tell me who really built it. The park was in bad condition and almost impossible to skate, but you could still imagine the might and beauty it once had." (Johannes Hempel)

2/3   Ulaanbaatar Skatepark | Ulaanbaatar.
         Photographer: Johannes Hempel
"Two years later in 2004 I came back together with a group of professional skateboarders to revisit the park. The skatepark was gone. Torn down three weeks before our arrival. Just one little piece was left. Like a monument of a crazy idea. During our one month stay we tried to find out where the park came from. We got almost as many stories as people we asked. It's been a myth and it stayed one." (Johannes Hempel)

10   Ulaanbaatar Skatepark | Ulaanbaatar | Summer 2002.
         Photographer: Johannes Hempel

12/13   Airport road and power plant | Ulaanbaatar.
         Photographer: Bertrand Trichet

14/15   Downtown Ulaanbaatar.
         Photographer: Pontus Alv

16/17   A street uptown after one day of rain | Ulaanbaatar.
         Photographer: Pontus Alv

18/19   Downtown Ulaanbaatar.
         Photographer: Pontus Alv

20/21   Suburbs | Ulaanbaatar.
         Photographer: Henrik Edelbo

22   Scott Bourne | Wallride | Ulaanbaatar.
         Photographer: Pontus Alv
"Again… This thing was basically dirt. Not only that, but if your board shot out it went directly into traffic. This thing was almost impossible to skate for a number of reasons that are probably pretty visible, but in the end it was one of the best Wallrides ever." (Scott Bourne)

23   Uptown Ulaanbaatar.
         Photographer: Alexander Basile

24   Muki Rüstig | Ollie | Ulaanbaatar.
         Photographer: Bertrand Trichet
"After drowning the Mongolian soldier with the vodka we bought in the shop, the next meaningful task for Muki was to ollie the rail behind the store." (Chris Pfanner)

25   Geoffrey van Hove | Backside 180 Ollie | Ulaanbaatar.
         Photographer: Alexander Basile
"Luckily we found this almost perfect double set. Of course some crack in the landing, but Geoffrey pulled down a Backside 180 before we got kicked out." (Alexander Basile)

26/27   Kenny Reed | Backside 5-0 Transfer | Ulaanbaatar.
         Photographer: Alexander Basile
"This spot was in the chinatown part of Ulaanbaatar. We found it because of this ger somebody put just between all these skyscrapers next to the rail. Kenny Reed, 5-0 Transfer." (Alexander Basile)

28   Downtown Ulaanbaatar.
         Photographer: Alexander Basile

29   Pontus Alv | Ollie into the bank | Ulaanbaatar.
         Photographer: Bertrand Trichet
"When we arrived I immediately realized that the city was full of flat bank spots. Spending a month in Mongolia shooting and skating banks in almost every part of town, I kept on wondering about the reasons for this architectural phenomenon…" (Bertrand Trichet)

30   Top: Downtown Ulaanbaatar.
                  Photographer: Bertrand Trichet
         Bottom: Downtown Ulaanbaatar.
                  Photographer: Henrik Edelbo

31   Uptown Ulaanbaatar.
         Photographer: Bertrand Trichet

32/33   Scott Bourne | Wallride | Ulaanbaatar.
         Photographer: Bertrand Trichet

34/35   Power plant | Ulaanbaatar.
         Photographer: Bertrand Trichet

36/37   Julian Dykmans crossing the ditch | Airport | Ulaanbaatar.
         Photographer: Bertrand Trichet
"The day we landed in Ulaanbaatar, we directly spotted the ditch while driving out of the airport. That gave us a lot of hope on the quantity of spots in the city because this one looked amazing. It ended up being a typical Mongolia spot, which means rough, holes, dirt and uncertainty. It also ended up to be one of the best spots we skated." (Julian Dykmans)

38   Julian Dykmans | Ollie One Foot | Airport | Ulaanbaatar.
         Photographer: Bertrand Trichet

41   Pontus Alv | Ollie | Airport | Ulaanbaatar.
         Photographer: Bertrand Trichet
"I have always been into sketchy spots but every now and then you wanna skate something clean and easy. These clean spots don't exist, so after a while it gets quite frustrating. Each session was blood, sweat and tears and every trick you made was gold." (Pontus Alv)

42   Top: Julian Dykmans | 360 Flip | Airport | Ulaanbaatar.
                  Photographer: Alexander Basile
42   Bottom: Hugo Liard | Nosepick | Airport | Ulaanbaatar.
                  Photographer: Johannes Hempel

43   Vincent Gootzen | Nollie Backside Flip | Airport | Ulaanbaatar.
Photographer: Pontus Alv

44   First time at the Skatepark | Ulaanbaatar.
Photographer: Alexander Basile
"This day we decided to go all together to the skatepark. We already knew it was torn down, but we all could imagine how big it used to be. We entered from the wrong side, therefore we had to climb some fences..." (Alexander Basile)

45   Hugo Liard | Frontside Rock | Ulaanbaatar.
Photographer: Pontus Alv

46   Julian Dykmans | Frontside Crailtap | Ulaanbaatar.
Photographer: Bertrand Trichet
"We don't know precisely what had triggered the construction of the skatepark, but what we can say is that it has been built by un-experienced constructors and that they did it with the help of pictures from magazines (Thrasher Magazine probably due to the giant logo that was painted on one of the ramps) or the internet. The quarter was a good example, the surface was covered with a roof copper patchwork fixed with nails. The structure itself was done with recycled plumbing pieces. To make it short, it was the sketchiest and most dangerous ramp I ever saw." (Bertrand Trichet)

48   Julian Dykmans, Scott Bourne and kids | Ulaanbaatar.
Photographer: Bertrand Trichet

49   *Top:*   Scott Bourne | Frontside Disaster | Ulaanbaatar.
         Bottom: Scott Bourne | Ulaanbaatar.
             Photographer: Pontus Alv
"One quarter pipe still standing and it was janky as all hell. Bad runway, sharp metal lip, nails hanging out, no platform... You know, great fun! I can't believe some of the tricks that went down here. On this day I had taken off my soft wheels to try to do a Disaster on this thing. The ground was almost dirt and where the ramp met the earth was just as dangerous as where the ramp met the sky. At one point my foot slipped off and got snagged on the top of the ramp and I hung there by one foot for a few moments before my shoe lace broke sending me back down to the earth and Pontus' laughter." (Scott Bourne)

50/51   Uptown Ulaanbaatar.
Photographer: Pontus Alv

52   Uptown Ulaanbaatar.
Photographer: Pontus Alv

53   Hugo Liard | Ollie | Ulaanbaatar.
Photographer: Bertrand Trichet

54–59   Block series | Ulaanbaatar.
Photographer: Pontus Alv
"I remember at night we could see which flats were looking at the same TV channels with the lights changing at the same time." (Quentin de Briey)

60/61   Kenny Reed | Frontside Bluntslide to Fakie | Ulaanbaatar.
Photographer: Pontus Alv

62–73   KIDS SNAPPING

63   Class of the Independent School | Ulaanbaatar.
Photographer: Bertrand Trichet

"During our trip we did a project with a class from a school for disadvantaged children. None of us had any experience in this kind of work. Up in the mountains, in a gers and block-huts neighbourhood, accessible via dust roads, you can find one of these schools. You can find them all over the world, they provide kids and/or parents with a little aid, so the kids do not need to work and can actually go to school. The one we visited also had the particularity of including one or two handicapped kids with the rest of the class. We did not have a big budget to help them, but we did what we do best: talking about skateboarding and photography. Each schoolboy and girl was then equipped with a disposable camera for a photo-homework. They had to take pictures of their animal(s), best friend(s), family, house and something they especially liked. We've been totally impressed by their pictures and it was a hard choice to make a small selection." (Johannes Hempel and Bertrand Trichet)

64   Naranzul, 11 years old
65   *Top:*   Nandinzezeg, 13 years old
         Center: Badamzezeg, 12 years old
         Bottom: Soylendene, 13 years old
66   *Top:*   Altanzul, 13 years old
         Center: Altanzul, 13 years old
         Bottom: Zolzaya, 14 years old
67   *Top:*   Duegum, 14 years old
         Center: Altanzul, 13 years old
         Bottom: Amgalanbayar, 13 years old
68/69   Soylendene, 13 years old
70/71   Enkhbayar, 20 years old
72/73   Enkhbayar, 20 years old

74–83   DEMODAY

75   Jerome from Holland | Sükhbaatar Square | Ulaanbaatar.
Photographer: Lars Greiwe
"The skateboard demo took place on the Sükhbaatar Square, which is the main plaza in Ulaanbaatar in front of the Mongolian Parliament. The day was so hot, but still everyone was super motivated to skate. Maybe because we knew a lot of people would see skateboarding for their first time. Crowds were passing by watching for a while, then continuing their regular daily matters. For me, this demo felt more like the arrival of a travelling circus in town, and everyone was coming to watch it." (Alexander Basile)

76   Kenny Reed, Bayartuul Lundeg and Mongolian TV.
Sükhbaatar Square | Ulaanbaatar.
Photographer: Bertrand Trichet

77   Kenny Reed | Backside Smithgrind.
Sükhbaatar Square | Ulaanbaatar.
Photographer: Bertrand Trichet
"Heat heat with Sükhbaatar on hand watching our back in the main square. The trip was nearing end and it was the hottest day yet. Tired and dusty luckily I stopped at the chinese herbal massage house before the demo… Before which I could hardly walk. Skating the demo was super fun rejuvenated and loving it consequently I suffered minor heat exhaustion." (Kenny Reed)

78   Local kid | Ollie | Sükhbaatar Square | Ulaanbaatar.
Photographer: Alexander Basile

79   Geoffrey van Hove | Backside Tailslide.
Sükhbaatar Square | Ulaanbaatar.
Photographer: Alexander Basile
"This was during the demo, it was super hot, but we had good fun on the brand

new obstacles that Schützi had built for us. Sadly they only lasted a few days because he couldn't find quality wood." (Geoffrey van Hove)

80   Vincent Gootzen | Melongrab | Sükhbaatar Square | Ulaanbaatar.
Photographer: Alexander Basile

81   Chris Pfanner | Backside 180 Melongrab.
Sükhbaatar Square | Ulaanbaatar.
Photographer: Alexander Basile

82/83   Tom Derichs | Backside 180 Flip.
Sükhbaatar Square | Ulaanbaatar.
Photographer: Alexander Basile

85–101   Gobi desert and backcountry series.
Southern and Western Mongolia.
Photographer: Bertrand Trichet

"My *meilleur souvenir* of this trip is my first day in the Gobi desert (with Julian Dykmans), let's rather say my first evening. After landing with the plane on a track which was really not different from the rest of the desert, we followed our guide Tsend to discover an incredible landscape. We were a bit like kids going to the zoo for the first time, steppe as far as you can see. It was really amazing, especially when I thought about the fact that people live here all year long. Anyway, at the end of the day we were still in the middle of "nowhere" in the desert… And so, Tsend asked us where we wanted to put up the tent. At this time we realized we had to choose a place to mount our tiny tent into this immensity. After being shaken in the jeep all day we did a quick choice, we would end up in the middle of "nowhere" anyway… We chose a flat area with a 360° panorama view, not too far from the track (which was not really crowded)… Then we just had to wait for the sun to slowly disappear on the horizon. It might seem stupid, but it was one of my greatest sensations of liberty." (Bertrand Trichet)

102   Monk | Tuvkhun Monastery | Orkhon Valley.
Photographer: Bertrand Trichet

"The young monk seemed to be the only person in the monastery. He showed us all the way around. I took this portrait and the same one with a Polaroid camera. When I gave him the Polaroid, he explained us it was the first time to see himself in a color photograph. During this one month (July 2004) in Mongolia, we met a lot of people. Sometimes it was only for a few minutes, just the time to take a picture…" (Bertrand Trichet)

103   Backcountry | Western Mongolia.
Photographer: Bertrand Trichet

104/105   Road to Karakorum | Mongolia.
Photographer: Quentin de Briey

"A big part of the Mongolian population still lives the nomadic life. Nowadays some of the nomads move their camp with the help of mechanic horsepower. In the countryside you see their trucks heavily loaded with gers and possessions. To me the vehicles in Mongolia were traces of the communist times. It seemed like there was only one model of truck, motorbike, jeep and van…" (Bertrand Trichet)

116/117   Quentin de Briey | Backside 180 Flip | Karakorum.
Photographer: Alexander Basile

"Some days before we went on that trip to the countryside, we were discussing about taking our skateboards with us… The bus was small and we knew we would camp in the middle of nowhere… So there would propably be nothing but endless grass hills… And this little bank of course!" (Alexander Basile)

118/119   Scott Bourne | Bombdrop | Ulaanbaatar.
Photographer: Pontus Alv

"This was one of the very few spots that one could actually call a skate spot. With the occasional interruption of Mongolian drunks going crazy, a couple of sessions went down here." (Henrik Edelbo)

120/121   Flooded street | Ulaanbaatar.
Photographer: Pontus Alv

122/123   State Opera and Ballet Theatre | Ulaanbaatar.
Photographer: Alexander Basile

124/125   Uptown Ulaanbaatar.
Photographer: Alexander Basile

"They said you shouldn't go by yourself, it would be too dangerous. At night you'd better stay at home, "two tourists got stabbed by a cab driver a couple of days ago." The streets are vivid at nighttime and the smog that is so intense during the day seems to be gone. Small food shops, the smell of grilled meat fills the air, the youth gathers around the last illuminated pool tables, one of the tiny supermarkets is still open. The security guard keeps an eye on me with suspicion, shadows are flittering below a bridge, "beds" are being prepared. The night is muggy, but this will change in a couple of weeks. People told us there's an organization that collects the lifeless bodies of those who freeze to death in the wintertime, hard to imagine right now. With the cap pulled down you´re one of them, a smart move for a stranger. Everything important is kept in a rotten plastic bag. They pass me and attack two guys a couple of meters away. No robbery, must be something personal, one of them seems to be injured. It starts to rain, time to get away…"

"Near the end of the trip I took a taxi and spent two hours riding through the city shooting all different kinds of places that I had visited before during my endless walks at night… The engine kept running while I jumped out of the cab to take one photograph at each spot." (Alexander Basile)

126/127   Vincent Gootzen | Nosebump | Ulaanbaatar.
Photographer: Alexander Basile

"Six in the morning, it's still dark. Reason for the early wake up is to skateboard a location which can't be skated during daytime since there's too much going on. In my eyes the location reflects quite well how the streets are in Ulaanbaatar, rough, dirty, sewer system sticking out of the asphalt. I find it challenging to use these present circumstances, come up with something as far as skateboarding goes." (Vincent Gootzen)

128   *Top:*   Hugo Liard and Tom Derichs | Ulaanbaatar.
          Bottom: Uptown Ulaanbaatar.
               Photographer: Alexander Basile

129   Hugo Liard | Backside 50-50 | Ulaanbaatar.
Photographer: Pontus Alv

130   Uptown Ulaanbaatar.
Photographer: Alexander Basile

131   Chris Pfanner | Melongrab into the bank | Ulaanbaatar.
Photographer: Bertrand Trichet

132   Night shop | Ulaanbaatar.
Photographer: Alexander Basile

133   Pontus Alv | Wallride to Nollie out | Ulaanbaatar.
Photographer: Alexander Basile

"Pontus always had two boards with him. A small setup – which he carried around most of the time – and one with soft wheels and wide board – the dirt machine – that speaks for itself I think…" (Alexander Basile)

134   Downtown Ulaanbaatar.
         Photographer: Bertrand Trichet

135   Muki Rüstig | Gap to Frontside 5-0.
         Sükhbaatar Square | Ulaanbaatar.
         Photographer: Pontus Alv

137   Tom Derichs | Switch Ollie | Ulaanbaatar.
         Photographer: Alexander Basile
"Quality-wise one of the best spots in Ulaanbaatar, which didn't make the three meter run-up much easier to deal with. A lot of tricks happened here anyway." (Tom Derichs)

138/139   Muki Rüstig | Fronside 50-50 | Ulaanbaatar.
         Photographer: Alexander Basile

140–149   Cross series | Ulaanbaatar.
         Photographer: Pontus Alv

150/151   Uptown Ulaanbaatar.
         Photographer: Bertrand Trichet

152   *Top:*   Family in their yard | Ulaanbaatar.
         Bottom: The yard | Ulaanbaatar.
                   Photographer: Pontus Alv

153   Hugo Liard | Oververt | Ulaanbaatar.
         Photographer: Bertrand Trichet
"One hour of cleaning, a mixture of sand and dust on the last tar parts and the session was on. It still cracks me up when I think of Hugo's loop attempt." (Tom Derichs)

154/155   Pontus Alv | Backside Turn | Ulaanbaatar.
         Photographer: Bertrand Trichet
"For me, Pontus was the most impressive skater. He has spent time alone in a taxi in sketchy neighbourhoods just looking for spots. He skated, filmed, took photos and even processed his films at night…" (Bertrand Trichet)

156/157   Julian Dykmans | Rock to Fakie.
         The Woodmarket | Ulaanbaatar.
         Photographer: Alexander Basile

158/159   Muki Rüstig | Frontside Ollie into the bank | Ulaanbaatar.
         Photographer: Pontus Alv

160   Uptown Ulaanbaatar.
         Photographer: Johannes Hempel

161   Kenny Reed and Bertrand Trichet | Ulaanbaatar.
         Photographer: Johannes Hempel
"On the hot days you could smell them when walking along the road. If you looked into the ditches on the sides, there were dead dogs, cats and other road kill which were swept aside from traffic. This day, we were on our way to the market, it was pouring rain. Just after walking along make shift bridges made from various wood planks to cross lakes which were once side streets, we came across this distended dog. Shortly thereafter we saw a severed horse head lying on the ground across from men in trench-coats selling black market puppies. We knew we had arrived at the market…" (Kenny Reed)

162/163   Little girl playing | Ulaanbaatar.
         Photographer: Pontus Alv

164–169   Cross series | Ulaanbaatar.
         Photographer: Pontus Alv

170/171   Uptown Ulaanbaatar.
         Photographer: Pontus Alv
"There were many kids in the streets of Ulaanbaatar. A recent UNICEF report states that there are "between 3000 and 4000 street and unsupervised children" in Ulaanbaatar." (Bertrand Trichet)

172/173   Uptown Ulaanbaatar.
         Photographer: Pontus Alv

174/175   Factory road | Ulaanbaatar.
         Photographer: Pontus Alv

176   Four friends | Ulaanbaatar.
         Photographer: Pontus Alv

177   Skateboard kids | Ulaanbaatar.
         Photographer: Pontus Alv
"Pontus met the two little Russian kids, Alex and his friend, at the only ramp left over at the park. 14 years old, some of the few active skateboarders in Mongolia. They went to skate the quarter nearly every day." (Johannes Hempel)

179   Young monk | Ulaanbaatar.
         Photographer: Johannes Hempel

180/181   Johannes Hempel with a kid of the school class | Ulaanbaatar.
         Photographer: Alexander Basile

182/183   Hugo Liard | Switch Crookedgrind | Ulaanbaatar.
         Photographer: Alexander Basile

184/185   Scott Bourne | Boardslide | Ulaanbaatar.
         Photographer: Pontus Alv
"Scott going crazy on this one, it was the roughest thing ever and so was the run up. He ripped his T-shirt in two pieces and was screaming very loud, I guess the citizens were a bit scared…" (Geoffrey van Hove)

186/187   Chris Pfanner | Melongrab | Ulaanbaatar.
         Photographer: Johannes Hempel
"The greatest joy within this picture is the memory of what is not revealed. After Chris landed this Melon Ollie, the little monk smiled and rolled around on one of our boards…" (Johannes Hempel)

188/189   Pontus Alv | Smithstall | Ulaanbaatar.
         Photographer: Alexander Basile

190/191   Scott Bourne and kids | Ulaanbaatar.
         Photographer: Quentin de Briey
"We spent a lot of time in the streets with the kids. They seemed unbreakable, jumping on the board without fear…" (Alexander Basile)

VORWORT *von Scott Bourne*

Ich denke, dass das, was zwischen mir und Skateboarding während der letzten 10 Jahre passiert ist, „der Weg" ist. Was ich damit meine ist, dass Skateboarding sich nicht mehr nur um Skateboarding dreht. Es geht genauso um die Dinge, die unterwegs auftauchen. In Wirklichkeit ist Skateboarding nur der Treibstoff für das Abenteuer. Die Idee war vielleicht „ok, lass uns hier oder da hingehen, um zu skaten", die Wahrheit ist, dass eine ganze Geschichte auf dem Weg stattfindet. Diese Geschichte ist der Grund für mich, weiterhin Skateboard zu fahren, nicht weil ich will. Schon vor langer Zeit wollte ich aufhören, Skateboard zu fahren. Aus dem einfachen Grund, dass mein Körper mir sagt, nicht mehr Skateboard zu fahren. Ich habe ständig Schmerzen. Der Grund, warum ich all das hier sage, ist um zu folgendem zu leiten: Was das Buch betrifft, denke ich, dass es alles beinhalten sollte, das Relevanz für diese Reise hat, auf die wir uns eingelassen haben, ohne zu wissen, was uns erwartet. Ich meine damit, dass das Buch dem Leser etwas über das Leben berichten sollte, nicht nur über Skateboarding. Selbstverständlich ist Skateboarding unser Leben. Das ist das, was wir tun. Aber das Photo eines Skateboarders, der auf einer staubigen Straße durch die Ghettos von Ulaanbaatar läuft, ist genauso wichtig wie das Photo von ihm am Spot. Oft zerstören die Medien die Geschichte mit Ruhm. In der Mongolei gab es keinen Ruhm. Wir haben für jedes Bild hart gearbeitet und es hat das Leben eines jeden Einzelnen von uns verändert. Was ich hier sagen will ist, dass das Buch all diese wundersamen Erfahrungen beinhalten sollte, die das Verlangen danach, Skateboard zu fahren, uns gebracht hat.

DAS TAGEBUCH *von Scott Bourne*

1. Juli 2004 | Charles de Gaulle Flughafen, Paris – Frankreich

Die Anzeigetafel im Flughafen zeigt Kairo, Casablanca, Rom, Chicago, Barcelona, New York, Mailand, San Francisco, Berlin, Amsterdam, Togo, Singapur, Moskau, Peking, Ft. Worth, Montreal und ungefähr hundert andere Städte, von denen ich noch nie gehört habe. Ich richte meinen Blick auf die Tafel und versuche herauszufinden, welches dieser Ziele mein zu Hause sein wird. In den nächsten 48 Stunden werde ich in Paris, Amsterdam, Berlin und Moskau gewesen sein, um schließlich Ulaanbaatar, die Hauptstadt der Mongolei, zu erreichen. Die Gedanken, die einem am Abend vor einer solchen Reise durch den Kopf gehen. Das Erste, woran man am Morgen denkt, wenn es endlich losgeht. Die Dinge, die man im Kopf hat, Menschen und Orte – Geliebte, tot und verschwunden – so tief im Gedächtnis vergraben, dass der Versuch, sich an sie zu erinnern, sie nur weiter verschwimmen lässt. Du erinnerst dich, woran du dich erinnern willst, und oft entscheidest du dich, diese Erinnerung zu verzerren. Du bist soweit gereist und hast so viel erlebt. Wenn du nach all den unvergesslichen Erlebnissen und unendlichen Entfernungen zurück nach Hause kommst – wo auch immer das sein mag – sind selbst die Menschen, denen du am nächsten stehst, dir fremd geworden. Sie sehen anders aus – und du ebenfalls – und all die Sachen, die dir plötzlich so wichtig geworden sind, verlieren ihre Bedeutung, wenn du heraus findest, dass du sie denen, die du liebst, nicht erklären kannst. Deine Erfahrungen bringen eine Einsamkeit mit sich, die sich nicht in Worte fassen lässt. So stehst du da – die Hände voll mit wundervollen Geschenken, die du niemandem geben kannst. Allein, allein, allein.

4. Juli 2004 | Ulaanbaatar – Mongolei

Aus dem Fenster des Flugzeugs verfolgte ich den Sonnenuntergang, bis er sich in eine orangefarbene Linie verwandelte, die sich endlos durch den Himmel zu ziehen schien. Die Linie erstreckte sich soweit das Auge reichte in beide Richtungen und leuchtete in verschiedenen Rot- und Orangetönen. Unfähig in Flugzeugen zu schlafen, las ich weiter in dem Buch, das ich mitgebracht hatte und schaute immer wieder auf den Spalt aus Licht, der den Himmel wie in Flammen aus tausenden Farben erstrahlen ließ. Ab und zu formten die Wolkenformationen riesige Städte vor diesem einmaligen Hintergrund. Nachdem die orange-rote Linie stundenlang einfach nur gleich bleibend am Horizont hing, realisierte ich, dass unser Flugzeug mit der Sonne entlang dem Rand der Welt um die Wette flog. Der Gedanke brachte meinen Orientierungssinn total durcheinander und ich hatte keine Ahnung mehr, wo Osten oder Westen ist. Zuerst war die Linie auf der linken Seite des Flugzeugs aufgetaucht, also flogen wir wohl in Richtung Osten über Russland. Dann brach vor dem dunkelblauen Himmel der schmale Spalt aus Licht wieder auf und irgendwo aus dem Nichts ging die Sonne auf. Langsam ergoss sich der Sonnenaufgang über das Dunkel und ein neuer Tag brach an. Weniger als eine Stunde später hatten wir festen Boden unter den Füßen. Ich hatte keine Ahnung was mich hier erwarten würde.

4. Juli 2004 | Chez Bernard Café – Mongolei

Wir wurden am Flughafen von Juliane Schmidt begrüßt. Sie ist eine deutsche Archäologin, die hier in der Mongolei arbeitet. Sie ist jung und attraktiv und scheint sich sehr über unseren Besuch zu freuen. Ihre Begleiter waren zwei mongolische Männer, einer davon ein Politiker. Noch bevor wir den Flughafen verlassen hatten, erklärte er mir, dass am Tag zuvor Neuwahlen in der Mongolei stattgefunden und die Kommunisten verloren hatten. Für ihn, wie für viele andere, steht das Land nun ohne Regierung da. Vor der Tür bemerkten wir sofort zwei große Kühe, die gegenüber dem staubigen Parkplatz des Flughafens in aller Ruhe grasten. Wir warteten die nächsten drei Stunden darauf, dass unsere aus Deutschland geschickten Pakete für die Reise durch den Zoll kamen. Am späten Nachmittag erreichten wir dann Julianes Wohnung, wo sie mit ihrem Freund Jean-Mathieu lebt. Er arbeitet als Entwicklungshelfer mit den Einheimischen und hilft ihnen bei der Entwicklung von Landwirtschaft. Ihm zufolge sind die Leute nicht besonders lernbegierig. Anscheinend besteht ihre Ernährung fast komplett aus Fleisch, aber sie scheinen keine Probleme damit zu haben. Jean-Mathieu ist Franzose. Die beiden leben bereits seit drei Jahren hier. Wir aßen gemeinsam zu Abend und unterhielten uns, wobei Sie uns eine kurze Einführung in die Geschichte des Landes und der Leute gaben.

5. Juli 2004 | 3 Uhr morgens

Draußen hört man das Heulen der Rudel von wilden Hunden, die durch das Ghetto streunen. Alles ist heruntergekommen. Ich kann nicht schlafen. Heute haben wir den Buddhistischen Tempel hier in Ulaanbaatar besucht. Auf meinen bisherigen Reisen waren solche Tempel immer die heiligsten Orte, die man sich nur vorstellen kann. Aber dieser hier war so verwahrlost, dass ich es kaum glauben konnte. Vor der Tür wälzten sich zwei betrunkene Männer über den schlammigen Boden und fingen eine Schlägerei an. Ihre Gesichter waren von Narben gezeichnet und durch Armut und Suff entstellt. Respektlosigkeit auf dem Rasen des Tempels – es war dieser Moment in dem mich diese seltsame Depression traf, die über Ulaanbaatar liegt. Mütter schickten ihre Kinder zu uns, um um Geld zu betteln, dunkle Wolken kündigten den kommenden Regen an über diesem heruntergekommenen Tempel, den ein einst mächtiges Königreich erbauen ließ, das jetzt in

Trümmern liegt. Zerstört durch den Einfluss der westlichen Welt. Einer Welt, die diese Menschen hier nie erreichen werden, und die sie ebenso wenig erreichen kann. Von unserem Balkon sehe ich das verarmte Niemandsland aus Jurten und Plattenbauten, wo einst zu besseren Zeiten Paläste in die Höhe ragten. Ich will weg von hier, aber wo soll man von hier aus hingehen? Wohin mich mein Weg auch führen mag, die Mongolei wird für immer in meinem Gedächtnis sein, eingebrannt wie eine Kindheitstragödie oder der Raub meiner Unschuld. Das Gefühl wird brutaler mit jedem Mal, wenn mich der Gedanke erreicht – wie ein vertrauter Feind, der zu mir zurückkehrt. Aber irgendwie lebe ich weiter, laufe, spreche und lache ihm ins Gesicht, egal wie groß die Last meiner Erinnerungen auch sein mag. Der Nachthimmel ist übersät mit Sternen, aber ich traue mich nicht einen Wunsch zu äußern.

7. Juli 2004 | **Ulaanbaatar**

Gestern war unser letzter Tag vor der Ankunft des restlichen Teams. Quentin und ich trafen uns mit Juliane und Mathieu zum Mittagessen. Von da aus fuhren wir mit einem ihrer Freunde, der als Forstarbeiter tätig ist, raus aufs Land. Jerome – begleitet von einem Freund aus Holland sowie einem mongolischen Mädchen. Wir verließen die Stadt. Ich habe keine Ahnung in welche Richtung. Schon bald verschwanden die Slums der Stadt hinter uns und machten der ländlichen Gegend und ihren Sehenswürdigkeiten Platz. Schafe, Ziegen, Rinder und wilde Pferde leben überall wild in der Steppe. Manchmal stehen sie einfach auf der Straße und halten den Verkehr auf. Je weiter wir uns von der Stadt entfernen, desto besser fühle ich mich. Die Sprachbarriere lässt unsere Unterhaltung eher spärlich ausfallen. Als die Stadt völlig aus dem Rückspiegel verschwunden ist, kehrt meine innere Ruhe zurück. Vor uns tauchen Gesteinsformationen auf, die Berge und Täler formen. Das grüne Gras der mongolischen Steppe bedeckt den Boden hier wie ein feiner Teppich. Das Grün erscheint in vielen Farbtönen, einer schöner als der andere. Es zieht sich über die Hügel und Täler in die Berge hoch, wo es irgendwann den Bäumen Platz macht. Die dürren Bäume sind wie Punkte über die Berge verstreut und zum Gipfel hin spärlicher gesät. Rinder und Jaks stehen überall in Herden beisammen. Wir halten den Wagen an, um sie zu photographieren. Man kann den Jaks so nahe kommen, dass man sie fast anfassen kann. Sie sind etwas größer als Rinder und haben langes, buschiges Haar, das fast bis zum Boden reicht. Hörner ragen aus ihren dicken Schädeln und lassen die Tiere bedrohlich erscheinen – im Gegensatz zu ihrer angsteinflössenden Erscheinung wirken sie sehr ruhig und friedlich, fast schon demütig. Quentin und ich müssen über ihr seltsames Aussehen lachen. Entlang der Landstraße sehen wir Kamele und kleine Erdhörnchen, halten aber nicht extra an. Jerome erklärt uns, dass wir zu einem Fluss namens Tuul unterwegs sind, der für die Bewohner der Mongolei eine Grenze darstellt. Nach fast zwei Stunden nähern wir uns dem Fluss und Jerome hält den Jeep an, um das mongolische Mädchen bei ein paar Pferden abzusetzen. Zehn Minuten später erreichen wir das Ufer des Flusses. Wir müssen noch einen kleinen Bach durchqueren, der zwischen uns und dem Flussbett liegt. Meine Füße machen den ersten Schritt ins Wasser und es ist eiskalt – so kalt, dass mir ein Schock durch alle Glieder fährt. Ich fühle mich ruhig und sauber und ich wate langsam durch den Gebirgsbach, während die Berge auf mich herabschauen und das Wasser seine Richtung ändert, als es meine Knöchel umspült. Die kleine Insel zwischen dem Bach und dem Fluss besteht aus flachen Steinplatten sowie einem riesigen abgestorbenen Baum, der im Schweiß der Sommersonne grau geworden ist. Vor mir rauscht breit und stark der Fluss. Sein Wasser ist so sauber, dass es flach und ungefährlich aussieht. Als meine Füße das Flussbett berühren, rutsche ich aus in der heftigen Strömung und kämpfe um meine Gleichgewicht. Die gewaltige Kraft erinnert mich daran, dass ich ein einzelner Mensch bin, ein kleiner Mensch im Reiche Gottes. Überall um mich herum liegt seine Schöpfung, so wie er sie gewollt hat. In meiner

Vergangenheit liegen in Trümmern die Stätten meiner Niederlagen, über mir segeln die Vögel durch die grenzenlose Weite des Himmels als ob es der ungezähmte Ozean wäre. Ich tauche unter und will nicht mehr zurück, aber meine Lungen und meine Beine zwingen mich wieder aufzustehen. Mein Körper zittert, aber nicht vor Kälte, sondern von den Schatten meiner Erinnerungen.

Ein Stück flussabwärts sehe ich zwei Frauen auf Pferden auf uns zu reiten. Eine davon ist das mongolische Mädchen, das mit uns im Auto gefahren war. Beide halten an und sie kommt zu uns hinüber auf die Insel, während die andere Frau die Pferde entlang des Flusses zurückführt.

Während ich hier auf dem toten Baum auf der Insel sitze, scheint die Erde zu einem Stillstand gekommen zu sein. San Francisco existiert nicht mehr, ebenso wenig Paris oder Ulaanbaatar oder irgendetwas, das von menschlicher Hand geschaffen wurde. Nur ich, meine Freunde und der Garten Eden, so wie er sein sollte. Von Zeit zu Zeit sehe ich mein Leben in diesem komischen Licht und hier in diesem Moment ist alles, was ich kenne, die Erde.

Heute Abend bei Sonnenuntergang, als ich mit Quentin und Pontus auf dem Weg zurück zu unserer Wohnung war, schien mir die Stadt unwirklich – fast höllisch. Betrunkene Männer lagen ohnmächtig auf den Bürgersteigen und in den Seitengassen. Junge Mädchen mit kurzen Röcken und hohen Absätzen standen unter den Laternen in der Hoffnung auf Geld oder einen Ausweg. Ich sehe nicht aus wie diese Menschen. Ich laufe, spreche und denke nicht wie sie. So bin ich wieder einmal einsam. Und in meiner Einsamkeit ist Ulaanbaatar wie jede andere Stadt auf dieser Welt – ICH BIN ALLEIN – und gleichzeitig umgeben von Freunden, mit denen ich mir den Weg zurück zu unserer Bleibe im tiefen Ghetto suche, wo wir uns für die Nacht einschließen, als seien wir aus Gold oder Silber. Als seien unsere Leben mehr wert als die der Leute, die wir gerade ohnmächtig auf der Straße oder beim Verkaufen ihrer Körper gesehen haben. Aber wir sind wie sie – verloren und allein in den Ghettos der Menschheit.

9. Juli 2004 | **Ulaanbaatar**

Die letzte Nacht war unerträglich. Etwa gegen Mitternacht hörte ich einen dumpfen Schrei. Ich lag auf einer Matratze auf dem Boden. Ich war erschöpft und schon halb eingeschlafen. Dann kam der nächste Schrei und mit diesem wurde ich hellwach. Von da an drangen die markerschütterndsten Angstschreie in unser Zimmer, die ich je in meinem Leben gehört habe. Verstärkt wurden sie durch meine Matratze, die direkt auf dem Boden lag. Die Schreie waren so voller Panik, dass es nicht zum Aushalten war. Ich rief rüber zu Quentin, der im Zimmer nebenan lag: „Hörst du das auch?" Wir gingen beide auf den Balkon, die Schreie kamen aus einer Wohnung zwei Stockwerke unter uns. Sie hallten aus dem Fenster über die dunkle Einöde des Ghettos hinaus und wurden von der Fassade des gegenüberliegenden Blocks zu uns zurückgeworfen. Ein unglaublicher Schrecken lag in diesen Schreien, unmenschlich und voll nackter Panik.

Über und unter uns streckten die Leute ihre Köpfe aus dem Fenster oder kamen auf den Balkon, aber niemand unternahm oder sagte irgendetwas. Das Geschrei dauerte fast eineinhalb Stunden. Irgendwann hörte es für etwa zehn Minuten auf. In diesen zehn Minuten spürte ich eine seltsame Erleichterung. Mir kam der Gedanke, dass das Leiden endlich ein Ende gefunden hatte und mir war gleichzeitig vollkommen bewusst, dass dieses Ende der Tod gewesen sein könnte. Ich war verstört von der Tatsache, dass der Gedanke mir so einfach durch den Kopf gehen konnte und fühlte mich plötzlich sehr unwohl mit mir selbst. Dann ging das entsetzliche Schreien wieder los, genau wie vorher. Ich zog mich an und war fest entschlossen runter zu gehen und an die Tür der Wohnung zu klopfen. Während ich meine Klamotten überstreifte sah Quentin mich mit angsterfülltem Blick an: „Was willst du machen?? – Du kannst da nicht einfach runter gehen!!!" Es war

197

nicht schwer, mir die Sache wieder auszureden. Aber als ich in dieser Nacht im Bett lag und die Schreie im Dunkeln langsam schwächer werden hörte, spürte ich eine große Enttäuschung über mich selbst und Quentin. Was hat es zu bedeuten, wenn jemand so laut schreit und niemand kommt? Es war ein Hilfeschrei, jemand schrie verzweifelt um sein Leben. Was, wenn das meine Schreie gewesen wären oder die eines geliebten Menschen – und niemand kommt und unternimmt etwas? Wovor haben wir eigentlich Angst? Ist unsere eigene Sicherheit nicht selbstsüchtig? Als ich so eine weitere Nacht schlaflos dalag, konnte ich nicht anders als an die Nazis und ihre Verbrechen gegen die Menschheit zu denken. Verbrechen, die ignoriert wurden. So etwas zu ignorieren ist in gewisser Weise genau so schlimm wie diese Verbrechen zu begehen. Ich fühle mich oft allein. Mir ist bewusst, dass meine eigene Sichtweise nicht immer die beste ist, aber irgendwie ist es für mich ein instinktives Bedürfnis, jemandem zu helfen, der laut um Hilfe ruft. Und wenn man nicht helfen will, muss man schon zu einigen Mitteln der Selbsttäuschung greifen, um dieses Verhalten vor sich selbst zu rechtfertigen – aber was bedeutet es, einen Impuls der Hilfeleistung zu unterdrücken? Ich fühle mich sehr fremd hier. Ich habe mich noch nie so anders als die Leute um mich herum gefühlt wie hier. Ich fühle mich hier weiter entfernt von den Menschen, als es bei den Amerikanern je der Fall war – und zum ersten Mal in meinem Leben bin ich froh, ein Amerikaner zu sein. Obwohl ich dem American Way nicht zustimme, ich habe definitiv Glück.

12. Juli 2004 | Ulaanbaatar

Am Abend stehe ich auf dem Balkon und beobachte, wie der nukleare Sonnenuntergang die Stadt färbt. Kleine Nomadenhütten stehen im Staub direkt neben riesigen modernen Gebäuden. Es sieht aus wie ein abgebranntes Brooklyn 2004. Ein Mann mit seinem Kind kommt auf einem Pferd die Straße entlang geritten, als von hinten laut hupend ein Auto vorbeirast und eine riesige Staubwolke aufwirbelt. Der Mann mit seinem Kind scheint unberührt. In der Ferne sehe ich Kräne und Industrieschornsteine, die sich in die Luft entladen. Der Himmel bildet einen radioaktiven Regenbogen aus Orange- und Purpurschattierungen, vor demselben Horizont dreht ein Riesenrad langsam seine Runden. Alt und Neu trifft hier unmittelbar und brutal aufeinander, was für die Mongolen vollkommen normal zu sein scheint. In den Straßen dieser Stadt kann man leicht an einen Punkt gelangen, an dem man sich dafür schämt, lebendig zu sein – an dem man sich dafür schämt, ein Mensch zu sein. Und gleichzeitig ist eine kurze Fahrt raus in die Steppe alles, was man braucht, um seine Lungen mit frischer Luft zu füllen und sich wieder privilegiert zu fühlen, am Leben zu sein. Wenn es so etwas wie Schwarz und Weiß gibt oder Nacht und Tag, dann ist es nirgendwo so leicht und deutlich sichtbar wie hier oben in den bergigen Regionen der Mongolei.

14. Juli 2004 | Ulaanbaatar

Heute Abend haben Pontus und ich in unserem Appartement etwas zu essen gekocht und auf dem Balkon mit Blick über die Stadt gegessen. Zu unserer Linken die grünen, grünen Berge der Mongolei, vor uns der Horizont in dichten Smog gehüllt und rechts von uns die Ghetto-Plattenbauten. Die Unterhaltung war ruhig und entspannt und zum ersten Mal bewunderte ich diese Stadt und dieses Land. Für einen Moment schien alles still zu stehen – der Schrecken der Armut dieser Gegend wurde unsichtbar. Ich fühlte mich im Frieden mit diesem Ort und auch er schien mich zu akzeptieren – den Ausländer, den Außenseiter, den Mensch unter Menschen in dieser verrückten, wahnsinnigen Welt.

In den Straßen hier kommen mir die skurrilsten Gedanken. Die Kinder mit ihrem reinen, unbekümmerten Lächeln spielen in einer Schlammpfütze,

die der Verkehr und der Regen gebracht haben. Das perfekte Kleid und die hochhackigen Schuhe einer mongolischen Frau, die voller Eleganz durch das Ghetto läuft. Ihr perfektes rundes Gesicht und ihre samtbraune Haut erhellen die Dunkelheit der Armut um sie herum. Das Fehlen von Gewalt an diesem Ort hinterlässt ein hoffnungsloses Gefühl – es scheint, als wäre den Menschen hier alles egal, als ob keiner versucht hier auszubrechen. Dieses Gefühl der Apathie ist allgegenwärtig. Niemand kämpft für mehr, niemand scheint mehr zu wollen.

16. Juli 2004 | Ulaanbaatar

Seit drei Tagen spielt meine Verdauung verrückt. Ich habe Durchfall und starke Magenkrämpfe. Gestern traf sich unsere komplette Gruppe zum Abendessen in einem koreanischen Restaurant. Das Lokal war sehr schön und hatte einen kleinen Innenhof mit Blick auf einen der Tempel der Stadt. Ich hatte zum ersten Mal seit Tagen einen gesunden Appetit – aber nach einem Blick auf die Speisekarte musste ich feststellen, dass es nichts Vegetarisches gab. Normalerweise habe ich auf Reisen wie dieser kein Problem damit, etwas zu essen, das ich zu Hause nicht anrühren würde. Aber mein Magen war in derart desolatem Zustand, dass ich es für besser hielt, woanders essen zu gehen.

17. Juli 2004 | Ulaanbaatar

Diese Stadt ist so düster und widerlich. Gleichzeitig strahlen die Kinder hier mit ihren schmutzigen Gesichtern eine einzigartige Unschuld und Leichtigkeit aus. Vor ein paar Tagen war ich abends mit Lars unterwegs. Wir verließen gerade eine Bar, in der ich mindestens fünfzig Euro für Drinks mit den Jungs ausgegeben hatte. Es war ein netter Abend und ich fühlte mich gut dabei, eine Runde zu bezahlen. Aber als Lars und ich an der Straße standen und ein Taxi anhalten wollten, kam ein kleiner Junge auf uns zu. Er war höchstens vier Jahre alt. Seine Arme und Beine waren so dünn, dass sie aussahen wie kleine Stöcke. Er war barfuß und trug zerrissene Jeans und hatte kein T-Shirt. In seinen Armen wog er ein kleines Mädchen, das sich um seinen Hals geklammert hatte. Er hielt sie mit einem Arm fest, während er die andere Hand ausstreckte, um uns um Geld zu bitten. Dabei zeigte sich der Hintern des kleinen Mädchens entblößt der Nachtluft, gerade noch nicht reif genug, um verkauft zu werden. Aber als ich die beiden so vor mir sah, kannte ich ihr Schicksal. Niemals zuvor habe ich mich so unbehaglich mit der Welt gefühlt. Lars und ich schauten einander mit gleichsam hilflosem Blick an. Obwohl man mich gewarnt hatte, man solle diesen Kindern kein Geld geben, tat ich es trotzdem. Lars und ich beschlossen, niemandem davon zu erzählen. Aber ich glaube, es war eine richtige Entscheidung, und wir stiegen in das Taxi und fuhren tiefer in die Nacht hinaus. In der Dunkelheit des Taxis spürte ich Tränen über mein Gesicht laufen und obwohl ich sicher bin, dass Lars es bemerkt hatte, verlor er kein Wort darüber. Wenig später waren wir beide betrunken, vielleicht um insgeheim die Erinnerung an die Kinder aus unserem Gedächtnis zu löschen. Ich glaube, ich habe bisher nicht darüber geschrieben, weil ich mich nicht daran erinnern wollte. Aber jetzt, in dieser Nacht, kommt alles wieder zurück. Draußen auf den Straßen bellen die Hunde und ich wundere mich darüber, dass ich das morgendliche Zwitschern der Vögel von Paris gegen das Heulen der Straßenköter von Ulaanbaatar eingetauscht habe. Auf dem Weg von einem Ort zum anderen wechsle ich auch zwischen unterschiedlichen Teilen meiner Selbst. Zusammengesetzt ergeben sie den Mann, der ich bin – veränderlich – verändert, anders, ein Neuer. Aber nur ein Mann – nicht mehr.

Gestern Morgen bin ich früh aufgestanden und ging zum Postamt in Ulaanbaatar. Ich sollte die ganze Gruppe gegen acht Uhr zur Abfahrt für unseren Ausflug nach Karakorum treffen und wollte vorher noch ein paar Briefe abschicken. Ich war die vorherigen Tage ziemlich krank gewesen und wollte nicht wirklich mitfahren. Die Landstraßen sind insgesamt katastrophal und selbst in einem guten Jeep bekommt man die Schlaglöcher im Magen zu spüren. Teil unseres Ausflugs war das Kloster in Karakorum, das ich unbedingt sehen wollte, also fuhr ich mit. Die Gruppe verteilte sich auf einen Bus und einen Jeep. Ich fuhr einen Großteil der Strecke im Jeep mit. Was eigentlich sechs Stunden dauern sollte, wurde zu neun. Den Blick aus dem Fenster des Jeeps gerichtet, bekommt man die Schönheit der Mongolei zu sehen. Es dauert nicht lange, bis man den dramatischen Unterschied zwischen der Großstadt und der unberührten Natur spürt. Die Landschaft liegt in malerischen Grüntönen unter der Sonne und Pferde, Kühe, Schafe und Ziegen leben hier frei und wild. Flüsse ziehen sich durchs Land wie die offen gelegten Adern der Schöpfung. Die Erde wird wieder zur Erde selbst, frei von der perversen Interpretation des Menschen. Bei klarer Luft erstreckt sich der Himmel endlos in tiefen Blautönen und strahlendem Weiß. Vor uns liegt eine Straße, die ohne Kurven und Abzweigungen geradewegs zum Horizont führt. Es gibt hier keinen anderen Weg als vorwärts, da das Wissen um Ulaanbaatar dich davon abhält zurückzublicken.

Kleine Siedlungen aus Jurten und Gers tauchen am Wegrand auf und verschwinden wieder im Rückspiegel, bis sich der löchrige, alte Asphalt irgendwann zu Staub und Erde verwandelt. Obwohl es einen dazu zwingt, langsamer zu fahren, muss ich zugeben, dass sich dieser Belag um einiges glatter anfühlt, als die meisten Teerstraßen, die wir bisher kennen gelernt hatten. Ich bin überrascht, als wir nach etwa zwei Stunden auf staubigem Untergrund wieder eine gepflasterte Straße erreichen, eine Straße ganz anders als die vorherigen. Diese hier ist sehr glatt, fast perfekt, und so kann unser Fahrzeug ca. eine Stunde lang bei durchaus normaler Geschwindigkeit vorankommen. Bis der Straßenbelag – und wie könnte es anders sein – irgendwann wieder komplett hinüber ist.

Unsere Reise hatte uns entlang des Randes der Wüste Gobi geführt. Die meiste Zeit war es elend heiß, ein konstanter Wasserkonsum, ohne zu urinieren. Die letzte Stunde der Fahrt verbringe ich im Bus, der besser gefedert ist und mehr Platz bietet.

Als der Bus Karakorum erreicht, sehe ich das Kloster Erdene-Zuu, das nicht von der Herrschaft der Kommunisten zerstört wurde, im Gegensatz zu den Mönchen, die ihren Widerstand mit dem Leben bezahlen mussten. Eine hohe, mächtige Mauer umgibt das komplette Kloster und vermittelt ein unmittelbares Gefühl von Widerstand und spiritueller Freiheit. Ich frage mich, welcher Gott diesen Mönchen zur Seite gestanden hat bei ihrem Widerstand gegen die Herrschaft der Kommunisten.

Während man an dem Kloster vorbeifährt, bemerkt man das Tal, das einen umgibt. Überall um uns herum erstrecken sich riesige, grüne Hügel und Berge, auf denen vereinzelt grasende Schafe, Kühe, Ziegen und Pferde wie kleine Flecken verteilt sind. In der Mitte des Tals liegt ein Dorf. Unser Bus erreicht schließlich eine kleine Zeltsiedlung. Wir verteilen unsere Taschen schnell in separate Jurten und eilen zum Fluss, um vor Sonnenuntergang noch etwas schwimmen zu gehen. In dieser Nacht schlafe ich zum ersten Mal auf dieser Reise tief und fest. Ich bin überwältigt von der Erkenntnis, wie spirituell und rein dieser Ort ist. Ich bin sicher, dass dies der schönste Ort ist, zu dem mich meine bisherigen Reisen geführt haben – nicht nur wegen der wundervollen Eindrücke, die dem Auge hier geboten werden – sondern wegen dem, was man in Herz und Seele zu spüren bekommt.

Wir haben für den Rückweg aus Karakorum nur sechs Stunden gebraucht – drei Stunden weniger als für die Hinreise. Kenny und ich haben gestern den kompletten Tag damit verbracht, kreuz und quer durch die Stadt zu laufen, um alle Bestandteile für ein Visum für unsere spontane Rückreise durch Russland zusammenzutragen. Nach drei Besuchen auf der Botschaft wurden wir ein weiteres Mal abgewiesen. Sie sagten, wir sollen morgen wieder kommen. Heute haben wir endlich alle nötigen Dokumente und Fahrkarten für die Reise – wenn sie uns wieder das Visum verweigern, sind sie einfach nur hasserfüllte Leute. Ich habe jetzt seit über zwei Wochen andauernd Durchfall gehabt und sichtlich abgenommen. Obwohl ich hier eine Menge unglaublicher Erfahrungen gemacht habe – ich kann es kaum erwarten, dieses Land zu verlassen. Draußen verbrennt die Hitze die Straßen und verwandelt diese Stadt in die Wüste, die sie eigentlich sein sollte.

Den letzten Abend in Ulaanbaatar verbrachte ich mit der ganzen Gruppe bei einem guten Abendessen im Taj Mahal, einem indischen Restaurant hier in der Stadt. Die Unterhaltungen waren sehr angeregt und drehten sich hauptsächlich um unsere gemeinsame Zeit hier. Während ich meinen Blick über die siebzehn Gesichter an unserem Tisch wandern ließ, sah ich all meine kleinen Erlebnisse mit jedem aus der Gruppe. Als ich sie so anstarrte, wurde mir bewusst, dass uns von jetzt an eine gewaltige gemeinsame Erfahrung verbinden würde, die wir alle noch gar nicht richtig realisiert haben. Erst der Lauf der Zeit wird jeden Einzelnen von uns dazu bringen, sich auf seine Weise an diese Reise zu erinnern. Die Summe dieser Erinnerungen ergibt unsere gemeinsame Erfahrung. Ich versuchte, mir meine Stücke der Reise vorzustellen, die ich selbst erlebt, aber nicht selbst gesehen habe. Genauso wie ich Szenen aus dem Leben anderer gesehen habe, die sie selbst nicht sehen konnten. Ich erkannte, dass diese Erfahrungen mich in so kurzer Zeit so nah mit diesen Menschen zusammen gebracht haben, dass es egal ist, ob ich jemals einen von ihnen wiedersehe – ihre Gesichter verbleiben eingebrannt in mein Gedächtnis – bis an das Ende meiner Tage.

Ich verließ das Restaurant vor den anderen und sagte verhalten und unverbindlich Lebewohl. Ich bin kein Freund von großen Abschieden oder dem Gedanken an einen endgültigen Schlussstrich. Am Ende eines großartigen Romans weiß ich mit Sicherheit, dass der Autor, nachdem er das Wort „ENDE" unter seine Zeilen gesetzt hat, mit seinem Leben weitermacht. Und egal, wie viele Narben seine Erfahrungen hinterlassen und wie sehr ihn das Niederschreiben seiner Erlebnisse auch verändert haben mag, ist es doch unausweichlich und bloß eine Frage der Zeit, bis er wieder zum Stift greift. Auf der Fahrt zurück zu unserer Wohnung dachte ich daran, was Juliane über die Veränderungen hier erzählt hatte – wie sehr Ulaanbaatar sich verändert hat in den Jahren, in denen sie hier ist. Ich schaute aus dem Fenster des Taxis. Vor mir pulsierte der Herzschlag der Autos, die sich gegenseitig anhupten, die vielen Straßen voller Scheinwerfer und Menschen, die diese staubigen Straßen auf ihrem weichen fleischigen Selbst überquerten. Ich konnte nicht anders als mir vorzustellen, wie sich aus all diesen ärmlich konstruierten Gebäuden moderne Wolkenkratzer entwickeln werden. Wie das nächste Hongkong, das nächste Tokio, die nächste ZIVILISATION aus dem Staub emporwachsen wird, um sich selbst zu zerstören – ein weiterer Neonzirkus ins Angesicht der Erde geschnitten – eine weiterer wertloser Ort auf diesem Planeten. Aber so wie es in diesem Moment vor mir lag, hatte es seine eigene seltsame Schönheit. Ich fühlte mich privilegiert, diese Schönheit sehen zu dürfen, und war gleichzeitig erleichtert, ihr endlich zu entfliehen.

PRÉFACE *de Scott Bourne*

Depuis une dizaine d'années, j'ai pris conscience de l'importance du Voyage dans le skateboard. Ce que je veux dire, c'est que le Skateboard, c'est plus qu'une simple planche à roulettes. C'est aussi toutes ces autres choses qui arrivent au fil d'un voyage. En fait, le skateboard est le carburant pour partir à l'aventure. Peut-être que la proposition de base est : « Allons skater ici, ou alors là », mais la vérité, c'est qu'il y a toute une histoire qui s'instaure durant le voyage en lui-même. Et si je continue encore à skater, c'est à cause de cette histoire-là. Il y a longtemps que l'envie de faire du skate m'a quitté, pour la simple et bonne raison que mon corps n'a de cesse de me dire d'arrêter. Je souffre continuellement. La raison pour laquelle je raconte tout cela, c'est pour en arriver là : Dans ce livre, je pense que nous devons inclure tout ce qui a un rapport avec ce voyage dans lequel nous nous sommes embarqués, sans vraiment savoir ce que nous allions trouver au bout du compte. Ce livre doit parler essentiellement de la vie et pas seulement de skateboard. Bien entendu le skateboard c'est notre vie. C'est ce qui nous anime. Mais la photo d'un skater marchant dans les ghettos d'Ulaanbaatar le long des rues poussiéreuses est tout aussi importante qu'une photo de lui sur un spot. Les médias détruisent souvent le récit avec la gloire. Eh bien, il n'y avait pas de gloire en Mongolie. Nous avons travaillé dur pour chaque image et je suis certain que la vie de chacun d'entre nous s'en est trouvée changée. Donc, pour moi, cet ouvrage devrait inclure toutes ces étranges expériences auxquelles le désir de skater nous a conduits.

LE JOURNAL *de Scott Bourne*

1er juillet 2004 | **Aéroport Charles de Gaulle, Paris – France**

Sur le tableau des départs : Le Caire, Casablanca, Rome, Chicago, Barcelone, New York, Milan, San Francisco, Berlin, Amsterdam, Singapour, Moscou, Pékin, Ft. Worth, Montréal et encore une bonne centaine d'autres villes dont je n'ai jamais entendu parler. Je regarde avec attention cette liste et essaie de deviner laquelle de ces destinations sera la mienne, laquelle mène à ma maison, chez moi. Les prochaines 48 heures vont me conduire à Paris, Amsterdam, Berlin, Moscou et finalement Ulaanbaatar en Mongolie. Les pensées qui traversent mon esprit lorsque l'on s'allonge le soir, avant de s'endormir, la veille de l'un de ces voyages, les premières pensées que l'on a lorsque l'on se réveille le lendemain matin … Ces choses que l'on a dans la tête, les lieux, les gens – aimés, morts ou partis – sont si profondément ancrés dans la mémoire que le fait de tenter de s'en souvenir provoque leur distorsion. Les choses dont on se souvient, on les a choisies et souvent, on choisit aussi de déformer ce souvenir. Quand on a voyagé si loin et expérimenté tant de choses, il arrive souvent lorsque l'on rentre à la maison – où que ce soit –, qu'on ne puisse plus se fier aux personnes, même les plus proches. Elles semblent différentes, comme on l'est nous-même, et ce qui semblait si important devient anodin quand on réalise que l'on ne peut pas l'expliquer à ceux qu'on aime. L'expérience engendre une certaine solitude qu'il devient doucement inutile d'exprimer. On est là, avec tous ces merveilleux cadeaux que l'on ne peut pas offrir. Seul, seul, seul.

4 juillet 2004 | **Ulaanbaatar – Mongolie**

Je regarde le soleil se coucher par mon hublot jusqu'à ce qu'une ligne orangée, qui semble infinie, apparaisse en travers du ciel. La ligne s'étire aussi loin que l'œil puisse aller dans n'importe quelle direction et dans des nuances infinies d'orange et de rouge, et reste suspendue, là. Incapable de dormir en avion, je continue la lecture du livre que j'ai amené avec moi, jetant de temps à autre un œil à travers le hublot sur cette ligne brillante accrochée dans l'air, irradiant le ciel de magnifiques couleurs. Dans le même temps, les nuages à l'horizon semblent former des villes imaginaires dont la silhouette est soulignée par le coucher de soleil. Pendant un temps qui me paraît durer des heures, cette incroyable ligne rouge orangée reste accrochée dans le ciel et je réalise alors que nous poursuivons le soleil depuis le bord de la Terre. Cette idée fait exploser mon sens de l'orientation. Je n'arrive plus à savoir où est l'Est, où est l'Ouest. Finalement, cette grande ligne disparaît sur la gauche de l'avion : nous nous dirigeons vers l'Est, au-dessus de la Russie. Soudain, avant même que je ne m'en aperçoive, ce ciel, que j'ai regardé pendant si longtemps sombrer dans la nuit, semble s'éclairer et le soleil se lève, à nouveau. Lentement, la lumière envahit le ciel et l'aube apparaît. Moins d'une heure après, nous atterrissons. Je n'ai encore aucune idée de ce qui m'attend à la sortie de l'aéroport.

4 juillet 2004 | **Café Chez Bernard – Mongolie**

À l'aéroport, nous sommes accueillis par Juliane Schmidt. C'est une archéologue allemande qui travaille en Mongolie, ainsi que notre connexion avec la ville. Elle est jeune et attirante, et semble réjouie de notre arrivée. Elle nous attend avec deux hommes, deux Mongols. L'un d'eux est politicien. Avant même que nous ayons atteint la sortie de l'aéroport, celui-ci me dit que les élections ont eu lieu la veille et que les communistes ont perdu. Pour lui et beaucoup d'autres, la Mongolie a perdu son gouvernement dans ces élections. En sortant de l'aéroport, nous remarquons deux vaches imposantes, broutant les quelques herbes qui émergent de la poussière qui recouvre le parking. Nous passons trois heures à attendre aux douanes les paquets envoyés d'Allemagne pour notre voyage. En fin d'après-midi, nous arrivons enfin à l'appartement de Juliane où elle vit avec son copain, Jean-Mathieu, un Français. Il travaille avec les Mongols pour le développement de l'agriculture. Et selon lui, les gens ne sont pas des plus motivés pour apprendre. Bien que le régime alimentaire local soit presque exclusivement à base de viande, peu de gens semblent avoir de problème de nutrition. Juliane et Jean-Mathieu sont en Mongolie depuis maintenant trois ans. Pendant le repas, ils nous dressent un bref historique du pays et de ses habitants.

5 juillet 2004 | **3 heures du matin**

On entend à l'extérieur le son des meutes de chiens sauvages qui courent à travers le ghetto. L'endroit paraît être à l'abandon. Je n'arrive pas à dormir. Nous sommes allés aujourd'hui au temple bouddhiste d'Ulaanbaatar. Cet endroit a dû être l'un des plus sacrés que j'ai vus lors de mes voyages. Lorsque nous sommes arrivés devant le temple, je ne pouvais pas en croire mes yeux. L'endroit semble négligé. Plusieurs ivrognes se bousculaient les uns les autres dans la boue et se battaient à mains nues. Leurs visages étaient recouverts de cicatrices, déformés par l'alcool et la pauvreté. Manque de respect sur la pelouse du temple. C'est à ce moment-là que j'ai été frappé par l'étrange dépression que provoque Ulaanbaatar. Les mères nous envoient leurs enfants pour mendier, le ciel est chargé de nuages prêts à exploser et juste devant moi, ce temple décati, autrefois symbole d'une puissante dynastie qui semble avoir été détruite par l'influence extérieure des pays de l'Ouest, un monde que les Mongols ne peuvent pas intégrer et qui ne peut pas les intégrer

Depuis le balcon, on peut contempler au-dessus du terrain vague le coucher de soleil de la pauvreté sur un océan de yourtes et de HLM côtoyant le crépuscule d'une puissante dynastie passée. Je veux partir, mais où aller lorsque l'on part d'ici ? Quoi qu'il en soit, la Mongolie restera à jamais gravée en moi comme une tragédie de l'enfance, le viol de mon innocence, à chaque fois plus brutal lorsque mes ennemis arrivent à entrer en moi. Malgré tout, il semble que j'arrive à marcher, à parler, à trouver mon chemin et rire au nez de cette tragédie qui est aussi un peu la mienne. La nuit, le ciel est rempli d'étoiles, et je ne crains pas de faire un vœu.

7 juillet 2004 | **Ulaanbaatar**

Hier était notre dernier jour avant l'arrivée du reste du team. Avec Quentin, nous retrouvons Juliane et Mathieu pour le déjeuner. Nous partons ensuite hors de la ville avec l'un de leurs amis qui gère les forêts, Jerome, ainsi qu'un de ses amis Hollandais et une Mongole. Tandis que nous quittons la ville en voiture sans vraiment savoir dans quelle direction, lentement, les taudis disparaissent derrière nous et sont remplacés par la campagne et ses paysages. Les moutons, les chèvres, le bétail et les chevaux remplissent cette campagne. De temps à autre, quelques animaux errent sur la route et ralentissent le trafic. Plus nous nous éloignons de la ville, mieux je me sens. Les conversations sont perturbées par la langue. Une fois complètement hors de la ville, mon cœur et mon âme commencent à se calmer. Formations rocheuses qui émergent de terre et constituent des montagnes et des vallées. L'herbe de la Mongolie recouvre la campagne comme un magnifique tapis vert. La prairie s'étale sur les collines, les vallées et remonte le long des montagnes où elle laisse place aux arbres. Ces petits arbres se dispersent, de plus en plus épars jusqu'à disparaître en allant vers le sommet. Le bétail et les Yaks sont groupés au pied des montagnes. On s'arrête pour prendre des photos et on peut s'approcher si près d'eux qu'on pourrait presque les toucher. Ils sont à peine plus imposants que des vaches, avec de longs poils qui tombent presque jusqu'au sol. Les cornes qui émergent de leurs têtes sont fermement attachées à leur crâne, ce qui leur donne une allure effrayante – pourtant, malgré cela, ils semblent très calmes, paisibles, presque humbles. Quentin et moi-même rigolons de leur étrange apparence. Le long de la route, des chameaux et de petits écureuils ponctuent le paysage, mais nous ne nous arrêtons pas. Jerome nous explique que nous nous dirigeons vers la rivière Tuul, une frontière pour les Mongols. Près de deux heures plus tard, nous arrivons et Jerome arrête la Jeep afin de laisser la Mongole descendre pour aller voir des chevaux. Nous continuons quelques minutes encore jusqu'à atteindre les bords de la rivière. Il y a une petite crique que nous devons traverser avant d'arriver sur les berges. En mettant mes pieds dans l'eau, je sens un froid glacial, si glacial que je ressens un choc à travers tout mon corps. Je me sens calme et propre, j'avance doucement vers l'autre côté alors que les montagnes regardent vers le bas, vers moi ; l'eau change son cours alors qu'elle enveloppe mon corps. La petite île entre la rivière et moi est faite de longs rochers plats, et un grand arbre mort tourne au gris dans une coulée du soleil d'été. L'eau est si claire qu'elle paraît peu profonde. Lorsque j'entre dans la rivière, mes pieds dérapent avec le courant et je me bats pour garder l'équilibre. Sa force me rappelle que je ne suis qu'un homme, un petit homme dans le domaine de Dieu. Tout autour de moi, il y a cette peau, façonnée comme Il l'a voulue. Mon passé est peuplé des villes de ma propre perte – au-dessus de moi de grands oiseaux planent dans le ciel comme s'il s'agissait d'un océan sans fin. Je plonge complètement et je ne veux plus remonter, mais mes poumons et mes pieds me forcent à revenir à la surface. Mon corps frissonne, pas à cause du froid, mais de ces villes enfermées dans ma mémoire.

En aval, j'aperçois deux femmes à cheval venir vers nous. L'une d'entre elles est la Mongole qui a voyagé avec nous. Elles s'arrêtent sur la petite île avant que l'autre femme emmène avec elle les deux chevaux.

Je m'assois sur l'arbre mort ; la rotation de la Terre semble s'être arrêtée. San Francisco n'existe plus, pas plus que Paris, Ulaanbaatar ou quoi que ce soit fait de la main de l'homme. Il n'y a que moi, mes amis et le jardin d'Eden comme il avait été prévu. De temps à autre, je vois ma vie au travers de cette étrange lumière, et à cet instant, tout ce que je retiens c'est la Terre.

Ce soir, alors que le soleil commence à descendre et que nous revenons à l'appartement avec Quentin et Pontus, la ville semble irréelle, sorte de paradis infernal. Des hommes ivres perdent conscience sur les trottoirs et les ruelles. De jeunes Mongoles en talon haut et minijupe traînent, à la recherche d'un peu d'argent ou simplement d'un moyen de s'en sortir. Je ne ressemble pas à ces gens, je ne parle pas, je ne marche pas, je ne pense pas comme eux et je me sens à nouveau seul. Et dans cette solitude, je trouve que cet endroit ressemble à n'importe quel autre endroit du monde – JE SUIS SEUL – et maintenant, parmi mes amis, nous retrouvons ensemble le chemin du ghetto où se trouve notre appartement et nous nous enfermons à l'intérieur comme si nous étions du métal précieux. De l'or, ou de l'argent, comme si nos vies avaient plus de valeur que celles de ceux que nous avons vu sombrer dans les rues ou vendre leur corps. Pourtant, nous sommes comme eux, perdus et seuls dans les ghettos de l'humanité.

9 juillet 2004 | **Ulaanbaatar**

La nuit dernière fut insoutenable. Aux alentours de minuit, j'ai entendu un cri. J'étais allongé sur mon matelas, sur le sol, épuisé et presque endormi. Et le cri se fit entendre à nouveau. Cette fois là, il me réveilla complètement. Notre appartement s'est alors empli des pires hurlements que je n'avais jamais entendus. Les cris étaient amplifiés par mon matelas qui était à même le sol. C'était si intense que c'en était incroyable. J'ai alors appelé Quentin dans la chambre d'à côté. « Tu entends ça ? » et nous nous sommes retrouvés tous les deux sur le balcon. Le cri venait de deux étages plus bas. Il faisait écho sur l'immeuble d'en face à travers ce ghetto dévasté d'Ulaanbaatar, et revenait sur nous. Le cri était incroyablement horrible.

En dessous et au-dessus de nous, nous voyions des têtes sortir des fenêtres et des balcons, mais personne ne fit, ni ne dit quoi que ce soit. Ce hurlement dura pratiquement une heure et demie. À un moment, il s'arrêta pendant dix minutes. Et pendant ces dix minutes, je fus pris d'un étrange soulagement. J'étais envahi par l'idée que cette souffrance était arrivée à une fin, même si, dans mes pensées, je me disais que cette fin pouvait bien être la mort. J'étais confus de réaliser que je pouvais penser une chose pareille. Je sentis la gêne m'envahir. Puis tout à coup, juste comme avant, les cris reprirent. J'ai commencé à m'habiller, prêt à aller frapper à la porte de cet appartement. Mais tandis que j'enfilais mes vêtements, le visage de Quentin s'est empli d'une expression de terreur. « Qu'est ce que tu vas faire ? Tu ne peux pas aller là-bas !!! » Ce ne fut pas difficile pour lui de me dissuader, mais lorsque je me suis recouché et que j'entendais ces cris se dissiper lentement, j'ai ressenti une terrible déception envers moi-même et envers Quentin. Que cela signifie-t-il lorsque quelqu'un crie ainsi et que personne ne vient ? C'était un cri de détresse, un cri désespéré de détresse. Qu'est-ce que cela aurait été si ce cri avait été le mien ou celui de quelqu'un qui m'est cher et que personne ne soit venu ? Que craignons-nous vraiment ? Notre sécurité n'est-elle pas égoïste ? Une autre nuit sans sommeil. Je ne pouvais m'empêcher de penser aux Nazis et les crimes qu'ils ont perpétrés contre l'humanité – crimes que les gens ignorent. Ignorer de tels crimes est presque aussi terrible que d'en être l'auteur. Souvent, je me sens seul. Je suis très conscient que mon jugement n'est pas toujours le meilleur et pourtant il me semble qu'il est instinctif de vouloir aider quelqu'un qui appelle à l'aide et ne pas le faire provoque une certaine déception – réaliser que nous nous donnons plus d'importance qu'aux autres. Pourtant, que cela signifie-t-il lorsque nous arrivons à surpasser cette impulsion, cet instinct et aller aider l'autre ? Je me sens très étranger ici. Je ne me suis jamais senti aussi éloigné des gens dans ma vie. Je me sens plus éloigné de ces gens que je ne l'ai jamais été d'un autre Américain et pour la première fois de ma vie, je me sens chanceux d'être Américain. Même si je n'approuve pas la façon de faire des Américains, je suis assurément chanceux.

12 juillet 2004 | Ulaanbaatar

Dans la soirée, je me tiens sur le balcon et je regarde le coucher de soleil nucléaire assombrir la ville. De petites habitations nomades côtoient les grands immeubles modernes dans la poussière. Un peu comme Brooklyn après l'incendie de 2004. Un homme à cheval avec son enfant descend la rue, une voiture les klaxonne et accélère en soulevant un grand nuage de poussière derrière elle. L'homme et son enfant semblent imperturbables. Plus loin, je vois des grues et des colonnes de fumée se disperser dans l'air. Dans le ciel, un arc-en-ciel radioactif d'oranges et de mauves, dans le même ciel, une grande roue de fête foraine tourne lentement à l'horizon. L'ancien percute le nouveau dans un choc que les Mongols ne semblent pas remarquer. À marcher dans les rues de cette ville, un homme peut aisément se sentir embarrassé d'être en vie, d'être humain, et en même temps, il suffit de prendre une voiture et de sortir de la ville pour se sentir à nouveau privilégié d'être en vie, d'être humain et de prendre de l'air dans les poumons. Si le noir et le blanc ou le jour et la nuit existent, ils sont facilement visibles de cette hauteur – ici, dans les hautes régions montagneuses de Mongolie.

14 juillet 2004 | Ulaanbaatar

Ce soir, Pontus et moi avons préparé le dîner à l'appartement. Nous avons mangé sur le balcon, en regardant la ville. À notre gauche, le vert, les verts des montagnes de Mongolie. Mais en face de nous, l'horizon pollué par les industries. Et sur notre droite, les HLM. La conversation était lente et facile et pour la première fois, j'admirais la ville, la campagne. Tout semblait s'être arrêté pour un moment ; l'horreur et la pauvreté de cet endroit devenaient invisibles. J'étais ok avec cet endroit et il semblait m'accepter en retour. L'étranger, celui de l'extérieur, l'Homme parmi les hommes dans un monde fou – un monde fou.

Les idées les plus folles me viennent à l'esprit quand je marche dans les rues. Les enfants avec leurs sourires parfaits qui jouent dans des flaques apportées par la pluie et qu'une voiture a transformé en boue. La robe parfaite et les talons hauts d'une Mongole qui marche au milieu de la poussière de cette terre désolée avec tant d'élégance, son visage parfaitement rond d'une peau brune illumine les ténèbres de la pauvreté. L'absence de violence de cet endroit engendre un sentiment de désespoir, comme si personne n'y faisait attention, comme si personne ne voulait s'en aller. L'état d'apathie est particulièrement présent. Personne ne se bat plus – personne ne semble vouloir.

16 juillet 2004 | Ulaanbaatar

Je suis malade depuis trois jours, l'estomac. Violentes diarrhées et douleur constante au ventre. La nuit dernière, tout notre groupe s'est retrouvé pour dîner dans un restaurant Coréen. C'était un bel endroit avec un patio qui donnait sur l'un des temples. J'avais bon appétit pour la première fois depuis plusieurs jours. Mais lorsque le menu arriva, je réalisais qu'il n'y avait rien de végétarien. Lorsque je voyage comme cela, il m'arrive de manger des choses que je ne mange pas d'habitude dans mon pays, mais mon estomac m'a poussé à aller manger ailleurs.

17 juillet 2004 | Ulaanbaatar

La ville est si sombre et dégouttante alors que les enfants portent tant de légèreté et d'innocence sur leurs visages sales. Il y a quelques nuits, je suis sorti avec Lars. Nous quittons un bar où j'avais laissé près de cinquante euros d'alcool avec les autres. C'était bon et j'étais heureux d'avoir payé une tournée. Mais lorsque Lars et moi nous nous sommes retrouvés dans la rue pour prendre un taxi, un jeune garçon vint à notre rencontre. Il n'avait pas plus de quatre ans. Ses jambes et ses bras étaient si fins qu'on aurait dit des baguettes. Il était pieds nus, dans un jean déchiré, sans tee-shirt. Dans ses bras, il tenait une petite fille qui avait ses bras autour de son cou. D'une main, il la tenait, de l'autre, il demandait l'aumône. Les fesses nues de la fille étaient exposées à l'air de la nuit, pas encore assez mûres pour être vendues. Mais en regardant ces enfants, je savais quelle serait leur destinée. Je n'avais jamais été aussi embarrassé par le monde auparavant. Lars et moi nous sommes regardés avec le même visage perdu. Bien qu'on m'ait expliqué qu'il ne fallait pas donner d'argent à ces enfants, je leur donnais quelques pièces, et nous décidâmes de ne pas en parler. Il me semblait que c'était une bonne décision, nous sommes montés dans le taxi et nous sommes partis dans la profondeur de la nuit. Dans l'obscurité du taxi, je sentis quelques larmes couler sur mes joues, et bien que je suis certain que Lars les vit, il ne dit rien. Vers la fin de la nuit, nous étions complètement saouls, certainement en train d'effacer secrètement ces enfants de notre mémoire. Je pense que je n'ai rien écrit là-dessus parce que je ne voulais pas m'en souvenir. Mais maintenant, cette nuit, tout cela me revient. Dehors, dans les rues, les chiens aboient et cela me semble étrange d'avoir troqué les oiseaux du matin à Paris pour les hurlements rances des chiens d'Ulaanbaatar. J'entre et je sors de ces différents personnages. Et tous ensemble, ils s'additionnent et forment l'homme que je suis, changeant, changé, différent, nouveau. Mais seulement un homme, rien de plus.

18 juillet 2004 | Karakorum – Mongolie

Je me suis réveillé tôt hier et je suis allé à la poste d'Ulaanbaatar. Je devais retrouver tout le groupe vers 8 heures pour partir pour Karakorum et je voulais poster quelques lettres avant de partir. J'étais malade depuis quelques jours et fondamentalement contre l'idée de partir en voyage. Les routes de campagnes sont en très mauvais état, et même en Jeep, elles sont particulièrement désagréables pour un estomac malade. Malgré tout, il y avait à Karakorum un temple que je voulais absolument voir, alors j'ai rejoint le groupe. Nous nous sommes répartis entre le bus et la Jeep. J'étais dans la Jeep pendant la plus grande partie du voyage. Un voyage qui était supposé durer six heures et qui en fit neuf. À travers les fenêtres de la Jeep, la beauté de la Mongolie. Ça ne prend pas longtemps pour ressentir le changement brusque entre la ville et la campagne. Le paysage est peint d'une grande variété de verts, le tout entouré de montagnes. Chevaux, vaches, moutons et chèvres déambulent dans ce tableau, libres et sauvages. Les rivières tracent leur chemin à travers la terre comme les veines exposées de la création. La terre elle-même redevient la terre, débarrassée de l'interprétation perverse des humains. Le ciel est infini et expose ses bleus profonds et ses blancs purs. Un peu plus haut, une route unique s'étire sur toute la distance sans aucun virage, ou aucune sortie. Il n'y a nulle part où aller sinon tout droit, et la connaissance d'Ulaanbaatar nous préserve de regarder en arrière.

De petits camps de yourtes surgissent le long de la route et disparaissent à nouveau au fil de notre avancée jusqu'à ce que finalement l'asphalte usé et défoncé redevienne de la poussière et de la terre. Et même si cela nous force à ralentir, je dois avouer que la terre semble bien plus douce que n'importe laquelle des routes « goudronnées » que nous avons emprunté jusque-là. Après environ deux heures de piste, je suis surpris de réaliser que nous rejoignons une route en asphalte, une route très différente de celle sur laquelle nous avons commencé notre voyage. La route est très facile, presque parfaite et nos véhicules peuvent avancer à une allure normale pendant presque une heure, avant, bien sûr, de retrouver une route merdique à nouveau.

Notre voyage nous a emmenés le long du désert de Gobi. La plupart du temps, il a fait chaud et ce fut difficile. Consommation constante d'eau sans jamais uriner. Pour la dernière heure du voyage, je suis transféré dans le bus où je trouve plus de confort et un peu plus de place.

Lorsque le bus entre dans Karakorum, je vois le monastère d'Erdene-Zuu, qui n'a pas été détruit par le gouvernement communiste, même si les gens en étaient. Ses grands murs s'élèvent avec force autour du monastère et donnent immédiatement un sentiment de résistance en même temps qu'une liberté spirituelle. Je me demande quel Dieu était aux côtés des moines lorsqu'ils ont résisté aux lois du communisme.

Après avoir dépassé le monastère, on découvre la vallée dans laquelle on est entré. Tout autour de nous, ce sont de grandes collines et montagnes, leurs pâturages sont parsemés de moutons, vaches, chèvres et chevaux qui broutent. Un village s'étire le long de la base des montagnes. Notre bus s'arrête dans un petit camp où nous nous installons rapidement dans plusieurs yourtes avant d'aller piquer une tête dans la rivière au coucher du soleil. Pendant la nuit, je dors profondément pour la première fois de ce voyage. Je réalise subitement la forte spiritualité de l'endroit. Je suis convaincu que je me trouve dans l'un des plus beaux endroits qu'il m'ait été donné de voir, pas uniquement à cause de la sensation qu'offrent les yeux, mais aussi par le sentiment que l'on ressent dans son cœur et son esprit.

21 juillet 2004 | Café Chez Bernard – Ulaanbaatar

Nous sommes revenus de Karakorum en seulement six heures, trois heures de moins qu'à l'aller. Nous avons passé la journée à parcourir la ville dans tous les sens avec Kenny pour tenter d'obtenir des visas pour la Russie. Après trois visites à l'ambassade, ils nous refusent toujours le visa. Ils nous disent de revenir demain. Nous avons aujourd'hui tous les documents nécessaires ainsi que les tickets de transports, et s'ils nous refusent encore le visa, c'est qu'ils sont simplement emplis de haine. J'ai la diarrhée depuis maintenant près de deux semaines et j'ai perdu du poids de façon évidente. Et même si je dois admettre que j'ai vécu une expérience incroyable ici, j'ai hâte de quitter le pays. Dehors, la chaleur fait fondre les rues transformant la ville en un désert qu'elle était jadis.

23 juillet 2004 | Transsibérien – Mongolie

Je passe ma dernière soirée à Ulaanbaatar avec tout le reste du groupe autour d'un bon repas au Taj Mahal, un restaurant Indien. Les conversations sont intenses et toutes tournent autour de notre expérience ici. En regardant le visage de chacune des 17 personnes qui se tiennent autour de cette table, je peux me remémorer toutes les petites histoires partagées avec chacun d'entre eux. Je les regarde et je ne peux m'empêcher de penser que nous avons tous partagé une expérience formidable sans en être encore parfaitement conscients – seul le temps pourra nous révéler les différentes facettes de ce voyage, et les rassembler en une expérience partagée. J'imagine les morceaux du trip que j'ai ordonnés mais pas vus. Exactement comme si j'avais vu des scènes de vie d'autres qu'ils ont été incapables de voir. J'ai le sentiment que ces expériences m'ont plus rapproché de tous ces hommes en un temps si court que peu importe si je ne revois aucun d'entre eux, leurs visages resteront gravés dans ma mémoire à jamais.

Je quitte le restaurant avant tout le monde, saluant chacun parcimonieusement, mais sincèrement. Je suis effrayé par l'idée d'une fin, même dans les grands romans, je sais que longtemps après que l'auteur a écrit le mot FIN, sa vie continue, traumatisée et changée par le chapitre qu'il vient de coucher, jusqu'à ce qu'inévitablement, il reprenne son stylo. Pendant que je rentre à l'appartement ce soir-là, je repense à ma conversation avec Juliane où elle me parlait des changements par lesquels Ulaanbaatar est passé au cours des années qu'elle a passé ici. À travers les vitres du taxi, je regarde les palpitations incisives des voitures, les klaxons aboyant ici et là, les rues poussiéreuses remplies de feux et les gens qui traversent leur doux suicide de chair. Je ne peux pas m'empêcher d'imaginer ces buildings de mauvaise facture se transformer en gratte-ciel. Le prochain Hong Kong, le prochain Tokyo, la prochaine CIVILISATION à émerger de la poussière et à se détruire elle-même, un autre cirque de néons inséré dans la terre, un autre endroit qui ne mérite pas d'être visité, mais tel qu'il est, il a sa propre beauté étrange, une beauté que je me sens privilégié d'avoir vu et en même temps dont je suis content de m'échapper.

PREFACIO *de Scott Bourne*

Creo que lo que yo he vivido, acerca del skateboarding en los últimos diez años o así, es "El viaje". Lo que quiero decir con esto es que lo del skateboarding ya no solo va de skateboarding. Tiene que ver con muchas otras cosas que ocurren a lo largo del camino. En la actualidad el skateboarding es tan solo el combustible para la aventura. La idea puede que haya sido "vayamos aquí o vayamos allá a patinar", pero la verdad es que hay toda una historia que ocurre por el camino. Estas vivencias son la razón por la que continuo patinando, no porque quiera. Hace mucho tiempo que dejé de querer patinar, solo porque mi cuerpo me dice que no siga patinando. Me lesiono todo el rato. La razón por la que os cuento todo esto es para llegar aquí: En lo que se refiere al libro, creo que deberíamos incluir todas las fotos que tengan relevancia con el viaje en el que nos embarcamos, sin saber qué carajo nos íbamos a encontrar. Con esto me refiero a que el libro debería hablarle al lector acerca de la vida. No solo de skateboarding. Por supuesto el skateboarding es nuestra vida. Es lo que hacemos. Pero una foto de un skateboarder caminando por una pista de tierra por los ghettos de Ulaanbaatar es tan importante como una foto de él en un spot. Muchas veces la prensa destruye la historia buscando la gloria. Bueno, pues no había gloria en Mongolia. Trabajamos duro en cada foto que nos sacaron y cada una de las personas involucradas, estoy seguro de ello, el viaje les cambió la vida. Así que lo que quiero decir es que el libro debería incluir todas estas otras experiencias extrañas que el deseo de patinar nos trajo a todos.

EL DIARIO *de Scott Bourne*

| ### Aeropuerto de Charles de Gaulle, París – Francia

De pies en el aeropuerto, en la pantalla de vuelos se lee El Cairo, Casablanca, Roma, Chicago, Barcelona, Nueva York, Milán, San Francisco, Berlín, Amsterdam, Togo, Singapur, Moscú, China, Ft. Worth, Montreal y unas cien otras ciudades de las que nunca he oído hablar de. Me quedo mirando fijamente la pantalla e intento imaginarme cual de estos destinos es el mío, tratando de adivinar cual me lleva al hogar. Durante las siguientes 48 horas habré estado en París, Amsterdam, Berlín, Moscú y finalmente Ulaanbaatar, Mongolia. Los pensamientos que cruzan mi mente tumbado en la cama la noche anterior a realizar uno de estos viajes, los primeros pensamientos que tienes cuando te despiertas por la mañana. Lo que ves en tu cabeza, las personas, los lugares – a los seres queridos muertos y desaparecidos – lugares que tienes tan dentro de tu memoria que se distorsionan solo con tratar de evocarlos. Recuerdas lo que decides recordar y a menudo decides distorsionar esa memoria. Has viajado tan lejos y has experimentado tantas cosas que a menudo cuando vuelves a casa – donde quiera que esta esté – ya no puedes relacionarte con las personas que te rodean. Parecen diferentes, y tú también y lo que ahora se ha convertido en algo tan importante para ti, se vuelve un sinsentido cuando te das cuenta de que no puedes explicárselo a aquellos a quienes amas. Tu experiencia a menudo crea una clase de soledad que es imposible de explicar. Aquí estás con todos esos bellos regalos que no puedes dar. Solo, solo, solo.

| ### Ulaanbaatar – Mongolia

Estuve observando la puesta de sol desde la ventanilla del avión hasta que se convirtió en lo que parecía una línea naranja infinita que cruzaba todo el cielo. Mirando por la ventana, la línea se expandía hasta donde los ojos podían alcanzar con tonalidades de naranja y rojo y simplemente estaba allí. Incapaz de dormir en los aviones, continué leyendo el libro que había traído – echando un vistazo de vez en cuando fuera de la ventanilla a la brillante línea suspendida en el aíre que quemaba el cielo con magníficos colores. De vez en cuando las formaciones de nubes que cruzaban el horizonte parecían formar ciudades imaginarias que la magnífica puesta de sol silueteaba. Durante lo que pareció horas esta enorme línea roja y naranja estaba colgada del cielo y pronto me di cuenta que estábamos persiguiendo el sol a lo largo del borde de la tierra. Mi sentido de la dirección se bloqueó con la idea. No podía imaginarme donde estaba el Este y donde el Oeste. Ya que la enorme línea en el cielo caía hacia el lado izquierdo del avión y parecía que nos dirigíamos al este por encima de Rusia. Entonces, antes de que me diese cuenta, el mismo cielo que había visto oscurecerse a naranja, a rojo brillante todo a lo largo de la línea del horizonte – pareció que comenzaba hacerse más brillante, y el sol empezó a salir de la nada. Poco a poco la luz llenó el cielo y con ello llego el amanecer. Menos de una hora después estábamos en tierra. No tenía ni idea de lo que me esperaba fuera del aeropuerto.

| ### Café Chez Bernard – Mongolia

Fuimos recibidos en el aeropuerto por Juliane Schmidt. Es una arqueóloga alemana que trabaja en Mongolia y nuestra conexión con la ciudad. Era joven y atractiva y parecía muy feliz de nuestra llegada. Estaba acompañada de dos hombres de Mongolia, uno de ellos un político. Antes de que hubiéramos salido del aeropuerto me dijo que las elecciones habían sido el día anterior y los comunistas las habían perdido. Para él y para muchas personas, Mongolia ahora no tiene gobierno. Según salíamos del aeropuerto vimos un par de vacas grandes que rumiaban en la campa de enfrente del destartalado aparcamiento. Nos pasamos las siguientes tres horas esperando a que los de aduanas nos dieran el equipaje que habíamos embarcado en Alemania para nuestro viaje. A última hora de la tarde llegamos al apartamento de Juliane donde vivía con su novio Jean-Mathieu. Trabajaba con la gente de Mongolia ayudándoles en el desarrollo de la agricultura. Según él la gente es bastante reacia a aprender. Parece ser que esta gente tiene una dieta basada prácticamente por completo en la carne, pero no tienen grandes problemas con la nutrición. Es un hombre francés. Los dos llevan aquí unos tres años. Comimos y charlamos y nos contaron una versión resumida de la historia del país y sus gentes.

| ### A las 3 de la mañana

Afuera se pueden oír las jaurías de perros salvajes corriendo por el ghetto. El lugar está completamente descuidado. No puedo dormir. Hoy hemos ido a un Templo Budista aquí en Ulaanbaatar. Estos lugares son unos de los más sagrados que he visitado en todos mis viajes. Cuando hoy, pronto por la mañana, vi el templo, no podía creer lo que mis ojos estaban viendo. El lugar estaba tan abandonado. Delante de la entrada varios borrachos se empujaban los unos a los otros en el fango, para acabar a puñetazo limpio. Sus caras llenas de cicatrices y deformadas del alcoholismo y la pobreza. Irrespetuosos con las leyes del Templo. Fue entonces cuando la extraña depresión de Ulaanbaatar me golpeó. Madres mandando a sus hijos a mendigarnos dinero, el cielo encapotado con la inminente lluvia y justo delante de mi el ajado templo de la que fue una dinastía poderosa, la cual parece haber sido destruida por la influencia exterior del mundo occidental, un mundo que no pueden alcanzar ni les puede alcanzar a ellos. Desde el balcón uno puede ver la puesta de sol de la pobreza en una tierra malgastada por encima de un mar de detritus y proyectos de casas que convive codo con codo con la antigua y poderosa dinastía. Me quiero marchar ¿Pero a dónde ir? Ya no importa, Mongolia siempre estará grabada en mi mente como una tragedia de la infancia, o el rapto de mi inocencia, la cual se convierte en más y más brutal cada vez que el enemigo penetra en mi. Pero todavía parece que puedo seguir andando y hablando y encontrar la forma de reírme a la cara de esta tragedia, la cual es también parte de mi historia. A la noche el cielo está lleno de estrellas, pero no me atrevo a pedir un deseo.

7 Julio 2004 | **Ulaanbaatar**

Ayer fue el último día antes de que el resto del equipo llegara. Quentin y yo quedamos con Juliane y Mathieu para comer. Desde allí fuimos al campo con uno de sus amigos que trabaja en el tema forestal. Jerome – y uno de sus amigos de Holanda además de una chica Mongola. Condujimos fuera de la ciudad, pero no estoy seguro en qué dirección desde Ulaanbaatar. Con lentitud los barrios bajos de la ciudad fueron desapareciendo detrás nuestro y fueron remplazados por el campo y sus vistas. Ovejas, cabras, vacas y caballos rumiaban en las campas. A veces en medio de las carreteras ralentizando el tráfico. Cuanto más nos alejábamos de la ciudad, mejor me sentía. Las conversaciones son variadas debido al idioma. Una vez completamente fuera de la ciudad, mi corazón y mi alma comienzan a serenarse. Formaciones de rocas brotan de la tierra formando montañas y valles. La verde hierba de Mongolia cubre todo el campo como si fuera una delicada moqueta. Múltiples tonos de verdes. Todos igualmente bellos. Descansa sobre colinas y valles creciendo hasta las laderas de las montañas donde se convierte en árboles. Estos pequeños árboles salpican todas las laderas reduciéndose el número de ellos según te acercas a la cima. Vacas o Yaks forman manadas compactas por las laderas. Paramos el coche para sacar unas fotos, y a uno se le permite acercarse tanto a los Yaks que casi puede tocarlos. Son ligeramente más grandes que las vacas, con pelo largo que cae casi hasta el suelo. Los cuernos salen justo de sus cabezas donde están firmemente montados al cráneo dando al animal un aspecto fiero – a pesar de lo cual parecen muy calmados, pacíficos e incluso humildes. Quentin y yo nos reímos de su extraña apariencia. Más allá en la carretera podemos ver camellos y un grupo de ardillas, pero no paramos. Jerome nos dice que nos dirigimos al río Tuul, el cual es una frontera natural para la gente de Mongolia. Tras casi dos horas estamos cerca y Jerome aparca a un lado para que la chica Mongola salga a ver unos caballos. Después continuamos otros diez minutos hasta llegar al borde del río. Hay un riachuelo que tenemos que cruzar antes de llegar al río que descansa en la distancia. Cuando meto el pie en el agua me doy cuenta que esta congelada. Tan fría que noto como un calambre me recorre todo el cuerpo. Me siento tranquilo y limpio y poco a poco lo vadeo hasta la otra orilla mientras las montañas me miran desde lo alto y el agua cambia su camino para rodear mi cuerpo. La pequeña isla que descansa entre el río y yo está compuesta de rocas de río, largas y planas, y de un gran árbol ya muerto, teñido de gris al sudor del sol del verano. Delante de mi el río es ancho y fuerte. Sus aguas están tan limpias que parece poco profundo. Según meto el pie me resbalo con la corriente y lucho por conservar el equilibrio. Su fuerza me recuerda que soy un hombre, un pequeño hombre bajo el dominio de Dios. Todo lo que me rodea es su piel con la forma que él deseó. En mi pasado descansan las ciudades de mi desaparición – arriba están los grandes pájaros que navegan en el cielo como si fuera su intocable océano. Me sumerjo y no deseo volver a la superficie, pero mis pies y mis pulmones me fuerzan a ello. Mi cuerpo tirita pero no de frío, sino de las ciudades atrapadas en mi memoria.

Más abajo en el río veo a dos mujeres que vienen hacia nosotros a caballo, una es la chica Mongola que vino con nosotros. Se para y se queda en la pequeña isla con nosotros mientras la otra mujer conduce los dos caballos de vuelta al río.

Mientras estoy sentado, en el tronco del árbol muerto en la isla, parece como si la rotación de la tierra se hubiera detenido. San Francisco no existe, ni tampoco París, Ulaanbaatar o cualquier otra cosa hecha por manos humanas, solo yo, mis amigos y el Jardín del Edén. De rato en rato veo mi vida bajo esta extraña luz y aquí, en este momento, lo único que sé es la tierra.

A la noche – según el sol empieza a descender vuelvo hacia el piso con Quentin y Pontus – la ciudad parece irreal – incluso infernal. Borrachos desmayados en las aceras y callejones. Mujeres Mongolas jóvenes con tacones altos y mini faldas, buscando dinero o una forma de salir de allí. No me parezco a esta gente, ni camino, o hablo, o pienso como ellos y otra vez me encuentro solo – en esta soledad encuentro que este sitio es como ningún otro sitio en la tierra – ESTOY SOLO – y sin embargo estoy entre amigos, y juntos encontramos el camino de vuelta al ghetto de la tierra perdida de nuestro piso y nos encerramos en él como si estuviéramos hechos de metal precioso. Oro o plata, como si nuestras vidas valiesen más que las de aquellos que acabamos de ver desmayados en la calle o aquellos que vendían sus cuerpos. Pero estamos, al igual que ellos – perdidos y solos en el ghetto de la humanidad.

9 Julio 2004 | **Ulaanbaatar**

La noche anterior fue insoportable. Alrededor de las doce de la noche oí un tenue grito. Estaba tumbado en un colchón en el suelo. Estaba agotado y medio dormido. Entonces volvió el grito. Esta vez me desperté por completo. Desde ese momento en adelante nuestro apartamento se llenó de los gritos más insanos que nunca yo haya oído. Los gritos eran amplificados por mi colchón, que estaba en contacto directo con el suelo. Los gritos eran tan intensos que parecían irreales. Entonces le llamé a Quentin que estaba en la habitación de al lado. "Has oído eso" de ahí los dos fuimos al balcón. Los gritos venían de dos pisos debajo nuestro. Los ecos salían de las ventanas del apartamento al ghetto de Ulaanbaatar rebotando hacia nosotros en los edificios de enfrente. Los gritos eran increíbles debido a la naturaleza de su horror.

Debajo y encima nuestro vimos a gente sacando sus cabezas por las ventanas y los balcones, pero nadie hizo o dijo nada. Los gritos continuaron durante casi una hora y media. Llegado un punto pararon durante unos diez minutos. Durante esos diez minutos se apoderó de mi un extraño sentimiento de alivio. Me invadió la idea de que el sufrimiento había llegado a su fin e incluso en mi mente, consideré la posibilidad de que el final hubiera sido la muerte. Me confundió el hecho de que pudiera concebir semejante cosa. Empecé a sentirme intranquilo conmigo mismo. Entonces, exactamente igual que antes, los gritos comenzaron otra vez. Me empecé a vestir, dispuesto y deseoso de bajar y llamar a la puerta del apartamento. Mientras me vestía, la cara de Quentin fue invadida por lo que parecía una mueca de miedo. "¿Qué vas hacer?" "¡¡¡No puedes bajar ahí!!" No le fue muy difícil convencerme, pero según descansaba tumbado en la cama aquella noche – oyendo como los gritos poco a poco se desvanecían – sentí una gran desilusión conmigo mismo y por Quentin. Qué significa cuando alguien grita de esa manera y nadie viene. Era un llamada de ayuda, una llamada desesperada en busca de ayuda - qué hubiera pasado si yo fuera el que estaba gritando, o el grito de un ser querido, y nadie acudiese. Qué tememos realmente, y no es nuestra egoísta seguridad. Mientras yacía despierto durante otra noche más no pude dejar de pensar en los Nazis y sus crímenes contra la humanidad – crímenes que la gente ignoró. Ignorar dichos crímenes es de alguna manera un crimen igual de grande que el hecho de cometerlos. A menudo me siento solo. Soy consciente que mi juicio no es siempre el mejor y sin embargo siento que es instintivo en mi el querer ayudar alguien que me llama, y el no ayudar me produce un cierto nivel de propia decepción – una racionalización sobre la importancia de uno mismo sobre la importancia de otro, pero qué pasa cuando superamos un impulso o instinto para ayudar a otro. Me siento muy extranjero aquí. Nunca en la vida me he sentido tan lejos de la gente. Me siento más lejano de esta gente de lo que nunca me he sentido de los americanos y por primera vez en mi vida me siento afortunado de ser americano, incluso si no apruebo todo el sueño americano – definitivamente soy una persona afortunada.

12 Julio 2004 | Ulaanbaatar

Al anochecer me asomo al balcón y veo como la puesta de sol nuclear invade la ciudad. Pequeñas casas nómadas descansan entre el polvo junto a gigantescos edificios modernos. Parece como un arrasado Brooklyn del 2004. Un hombre a caballo con su hijo baja la calle mientras un coche toca su bocina y acelera levantando una tormenta de polvo detrás suyo. El hombre con su niño parece no inmutarse. En la distancia puedo ver grúas y volutas de humo desvaneciéndose en el aire. En el cielo se ha formado un arco iris radioactivo de naranjas y morados, en ese mismo horizonte una noria gira lentamente. Lo viejo se encuentra con lo nuevo de una forma que parece no ser percibida por la gente de Mongolia. Caminando por las calles de esta ciudad un hombre fácilmente puede llegar a sentirse avergonzado de estar vivo, de ser humano, y al mismo tiempo lo único que un hombre necesita hacer es darse una corta vuelta en coche al campo, para sentirse otra vez privilegiado de estar vivo, de ser humano, y de introducir aire en sus pulmones. Si existe el Blanco y Negro o la noche y el día, es fácilmente visible desde esta altura – aquí en lo alto de las regiones montañosas de Mongolia.

14 Julio 2004 | Ulaanbaatar

Pontus y yo hemos cocinado hoy a la noche en el piso y hemos salido a comer al balcón trasero desde donde se ve toda la ciudad. A la izquierda, las verdes, verdes montañas de Mongolia. Pero enfrente, el horizonte polucionado por la industria. A la derecha las casas estilo proyecto. La conversación era lenta y fácil y por primera vez admiré la ciudad, el país. Todo pareció detenerse por un instante; el horror y la pobreza de este lugar se volvieron invisibles. Me sentí bien con el lugar y él pareció también aceptarme. El extranjero, el forastero, el hombre entre los hombres en un mundo loco – mundo loco.

Las ideas más dementes saltan a mi mente cuando camino por estas calles. Los niños de sonrisas perfectas jugando en el barro que la lluvia a traído y que un coche a convertido en mugre. El perfecto vestido y los tacones altos de una mujer Mongola mientras camina por esta polvorienta tierra baldía con semejante elegancia, su perfecta cara redonda y suave piel marrón ilumina la oscuridad de la pobreza. La falta de violencia en este lugar le deja a uno sin mucha esperanza – es como si a nadie le importara, como si nadie quisiera salir. El estado de apatía aquí es como un colocón perpetuo. Ya nadie lucha – nadie parece querer más.

16 Julio 2004 | Ulaanbaatar

Durante los últimos tres días he estado malo del estómago. Diarreas incisivas y dolores constantes de estómago. La última noche el grupo entero se reunió para comer en un restaurante Coreano. Era un sitio precioso con un patio que miraba a uno de los templos del país. Por primera vez en días tenía buen apetito – Pero cuando llegó la carta no tenían nada vegetariano. Cuando viajo de esta forma estoy más abierto a comer cosas que normalmente no comería en mi propio país – Pero mi estómago había estado tan mal que decidí que debía comer en cualquier otro sitio.

17 Julio 2004 | Ulaanbaatar

Esta ciudad es tan oscura y repugnante y al mismo tiempo los niños llevan tan ligera e inocentemente sus sucias caras. Hace algunas noches salí con Lars. Nos íbamos de un bar donde me había dejado al menos cincuenta euros en bebidas con los chicos. Todo andaba bien y me sentía bien pagando una ronda. Pero en cuanto Lars y yo nos quedamos a solas en las calles para parar un taxi – un pequeño chico vino hacia nosotros. El niño no tenía más de cuatro años. Sus brazos y piernas tan delgadas que parecían palos. Estaba descalzo con unos vaqueros rotos y sin camiseta. En sus brazos sostenía una niña pequeña que se aferraba alrededor de su cuello. La sostenía con un brazo mientras utilizaba la otra mano para pedir dinero. El culo desnudo de la niña expuesto al aíre de la noche, todavía inmaduro como para venderlo. Pero sabía cuando miraba a estos niños – su destino. Nunca jamás me había sentido tan incómodo con el mundo. Lars y yo simplemente nos miramos con la misma cara de perdidos. A pesar de que me habían dicho que no diera dinero a los niños, lo hice, y Lars y y yo decidimos no hablar de ello. Sentí que había sido una buena decisión y nos metimos al taxi y marchamos – a la profundidad de la noche. En la oscuridad del taxi sentí lágrimas en mi cara y a pesar de que me di cuenta de que Lars las había notado, no habló de ello. Al final de la noche ambos estábamos borrachos – quizás tratando secretamente de borrar a los niños de nuestra memoria. Creo que no escribí sobre ello porque no quería recordarlo. Pero ahora – en esta noche – vuelve a mi. Afuera en la calle los perros están ladrando y parece extraño que haya cambiado los pájaros de la mañana de París, por los rancios aullidos de los perros de Ulaanbaatar. Entro y salgo de estos yos. Lo cuales todos juntos crean la suma del hombre que soy – cambiable – cambiado, diferente, uno nuevo. Pero solo un hombre – nada más.

18 Julio 2004 | Karakorum – Mongolia

Ayer me desperté temprano y encontré el camino a la oficina de correos de Ulaanbaatar. Supuestamente tenía que encontrarme con todo el grupo para el viaje al Karakorum y quería echar unas cartas antes de marcharme. Me había estado sintiendo bastante enfermo durante los dos últimos días y fundamentalmente estaba en contra de hacer el viaje. Las carreteras por el país son muy malas e incluso en un buen jeep son bastante desagradables para el estómago. Aunque había un Monasterio en Karakorum que quería ver, así que me uní al grupo. El grupo estaba dividido en un bus y un jeep. Fui en el jeep la mayoría del viaje. Un viaje que me dijeron que sería de aproximadamente seis horas, que acabaron por ser nueve. Mirando a través de la ventana de un jeep uno ve la belleza de Mongolia. No te lleva mucho sentir el directo e intenso cambio de la ciudad al campo. Los paisajes están pintados de tonalidades de verde con montañas por todos los lados Caballos, vacas, ovejas, y cabras rumian libres y salvajes el campo. Los ríos cortan la tierra como si fueran las venas de la creación. La tierra en si misma vuelve a convertirse en la tierra, ya no es la perversa interpretación de ser humano. El cielo cae infinitamente a través del aíre en profundos azules y puros blancos. Delante hay una sola carretera que se estrecha en la distancia sin giros ni salidas. No hay a donde ir más que hacia delante, conociendo Ulaanbaatar evitaremos que mires atrás.

Pequeños asentamientos de Yurtas, florecen alrededor de la carretera y se difuminan en la distancia, hasta que finalmente la bacheada carretera se convierte en polvo y suciedad. Pero a pesar de que le fuerza a uno a viajar más despacio, tengo que admitir que las pistas parecían muchos más lisas que la mayoría de las carreteras pavimentadas que habíamos conocido hasta ahora. Tras cerca de dos horas de pista estoy sorprendido de ver que hemos llegado otra vez a una carretera asfaltada – una carretera que no se parece en nada a la que nos recibió al inicio del viaje. Esta carretera es bastante lisa, casi perfecta y nuestro vehículo puede viajar a velocidades normales durante casi una hora, antes por supuesto, de que la carretera se vuelva a convertir, una vez más, en un mierda.

El viaje nos ha llevado por el borde del Desierto del Gobi. Durante la mayor parte, la cosa ha sido calurosa y miserable. Un constante consumo de agua sin orinar. Durante la última hora del viaje me cambian al autobús donde me percato que el viaje es mucho más suave y algo más espacioso.

Según el bus entra en Karakorum puedo ver el Monasterio de Erdene-Zuu, que no fue destruido por la ley comunista, incluso si su gente lo era. Sus altos muros se irguen fuertes rodeando el monasterio y le da a uno la inmediata sensación de resistencia a la vez que de libertad espiritual. Me pregunto qué Dios estuvo del lado de estos monjes mientras resistían las leyes comunistas.

Pasado el monasterio uno empieza a darse cuenta del valle en el que acaba de entrar. Todo alrededor nuestro son colinas y montañas verdes, sus herbosas costas salpicadas de ovejas pastando, vacas, cabras y caballos. Un pueblo se estrecha a lo largo de su base. Nuestro autobús se mete en un pequeño campamento donde rápidamente colocamos nuestros equipajes en Yurtas separadas y nos vamos hacia el río para nadar un poco antes de que caiga la noche. Esa noche duermo profundamente por primera vez en este viaje. Soy completamente consciente de lo espiritual de este lugar. Estoy seguro que es el sitio más bonito en el que he estado en todos mis viajes – no solo por la sensación que me dan los ojos sino por la sensación que llega a tu corazón y a tu espíritu.

21 Julio 2004 | ### Café Chez Bernard – Ulaanbaatar

Hicimos el viaje de vuelta desde el Karakorum en solo seis horas. Tres horas menos que el Viaje de ida. Kenny y yo nos pasamos recorriendo la ciudad entera intentando conseguir todo lo necesario para obtener el visado para atravesar Rusia. Tras tres viajes a la embajada todavía nos lo seguían denegando. Nos dijeron que volviéramos mañana. Hoy tenemos todos los billetes y documentos para el viaje – si nos deniegan ahora el visado es que simplemente son personas odiosas. Llevo ya dos semanas con diarrea y he perdido bastante peso. A pesar de ello he tenido increíbles experiencias aquí – no puedo esperar a dejar este país. Afuera el calor está derritiendo las calles convirtiendo esta ciudad en el desierto que debería ser.

23 Julio 2004 | ### Tren Transiberiano – Mongolia

Mi última noche en Ulaanbaatar la pasé con todo el grupo acompañados de buena comida en el Taj Mahal, un restaurante Indio de la ciudad. Las conversaciones parecen bullir – todas alrededor de nuestra estancia aquí. Según miro a la mesa a las diecisiete caras que se sientan enfrente de mi, podía ver en cada persona del grupo mis pequeñas experiencias. Mientras los miraba no pude evitar sentir como si todos hubiéramos compartido una experiencia alucinante de la que ninguno de nosotros todavía era consciente – solo el tiempo sería quien nos revelase y nos forzase a recordar el viaje en escenas separadas, que nos llevará a una experiencia compartida. Me imaginé los trozos de viaje que había representado pero no visto. Tal y como había visto las escenas de otras vidas que ellos no podían ver. Percibo que estas experiencias me han acercado a estos hombres en un periodo tan corto de tiempo que no importa si no les vuelvo a ver a ninguno de ellos - sus caras permanecerán a fuego en mi memoria hasta el final.

Abandoné el restaurante antes que nadie, dando delicados pero fáciles adioses. Me horroriza la idea del final, incluso en las grandes novelas, sé que mucho tiempo después de que escriba la palabra "FIN" – su vida continuará de alguna manera marcada y cambiada por el capítulo que acaba de terminar – hasta el inevitable momento que vuelva a coger el bolígrafo. Mientras volvía al apartamento esa noche pensé en los cambios que Juliane me había comentado en su entrevista – Los cambios que Ulaanbaatar había sufrido mientras ella estaba allí. Mirando por la ventanilla del taxi al incisivo palpitar de los coches, las bocinas ladrando atrás y adelante – las polvorientas calles atestadas de luces, y la gente cruzando sus suaves carnes suicidas. No pude más que imaginarme estos edificios pobremente construidos evolucionando a rascacielos. El próximo Hong Kong, el siguiente Tokio, la próxima CIVILIZACION en renacer del polvo y destruirse a si misma – otro circo de neón en la tierra – otro sitio que no merece visitarse – pero tal como estaba tenía su propia extraña belleza – una belleza que me sentí privilegiado de ver y a la vez aliviado de escapar.

A SKATEBOARD TRIP TO MONGOLIA

Verlag für Bildschöne Bücher, Berlin 2007
ISBN 978-3-939181-04-0

Production: Work in Progress GmbH
Executive Producers: Edwin Faeh & Oliver Drewes
Concept: Lars Greiwe
Art Direction: Alexander Basile
Layout: Christoph Merkt
Illustrations: Stefan Narancic
Words: Scott Bourne
Photography: Pontus Alv | Alexander Basile | Bertrand Trichet
Additional Photography: Quentin de Briey | Henrik Edelbo | Johannes Hempel

MONGOLIAN TYRES
A film by Henrik Edelbo
Motion Graphics: Stefan Narancic

Thanks to:
Edwin Faeh, Oliver Drewes & Peter Dericks (Vans) for making this project possible.
Johannes Hempel, Vision & Organisation
Andreas Schützenberger – IOU, Ramp Construction | Muki Rüstig, Ramp Construction
Scott Bourne, Textwork
Dirk Vogel, German Translation
Cedric Bihr, French Translation
Eduardo Sáenz de Amilibia, Spanish Translation
Sonja Altmeppen, Proofreading
Jochen Bauer – Playboard Magazine, Scans | Pontus Alv, Additional Scans
Bertrand Trichet, Color Adjustment
Henrik Edelbo, Filming | Geoffrey van Hove, Additional Filming
Julian Dykmans, Organisation Help
Tom Derichs | Kenny Reed | Hugo Liard | Vincent Gootzen | Quentin de Briey | Chris Pfanner
Bayartuul Lundeg, Organisation Help | Nasaar, Local Help | Purevsuren, Demo Permission
Juliane Schmidt & Jean-Mathieu Bloch, Help
DJ Jerome, Demo | Woodcenter of UB, Workshop | The Locals | Gambold, Footage
Giveaways: Carhartt Europe | Vans | Polaroid Europe | the Unbelievers | Yama Skateboards
and everyone else who helped us out, you know who you are.
Thank you!

carhartt®   BILDSCHÖNE BüCHEr

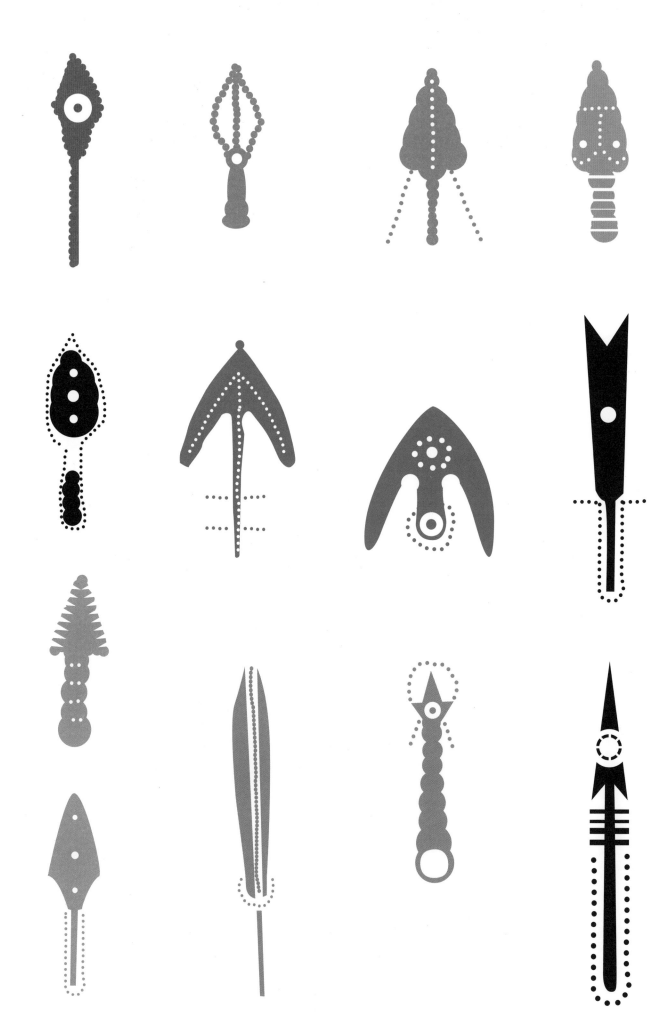